KILLER PARTY

Pretty twenty-year-old college student Katrina Montgomery got a lot more than she bargained for when she went to a party with Justin Merriman and his skinhead friends on November 28, 1992. At one point, Merriman pinned Katrina Montgomery down on a bed with his body. At first she giggled, but then she started screaming for him to get off of her. Others rushed into the room to find Montgomery crying and several skinheads standing around her menacingly. She was holding her stomach as if someone had just punched her.

While one of her friends escorted Katrina out of the room, the party's host asked what had happened. Merriman told him, "Nothin' happened."

"You sure?" the host asked.

"Yeah, I'm sure," Merriman responded.

The host cleared the room of all the skinheads, including Merriman.

After this incident Merriman told his friends, "I'm going to get that bitch!" As Merriman started passing out steak knives from the kitchen to his skinhead buddies, he said, "Get her."

OTHER PINNACLE BOOKS
BY ROBERT SCOTT

LIKE FATHER, LIKE SON

SAVAGE

ROPE BURNS

DANGEROUS ATTRACTION

ROBERT SCOTT

PINNACLE BOOKS
Kensington Publishing Corp.
http://www.kensingtonbooks.com

Some names have been changed to protect the privacy of individuals connected to this story.

PINNACLE BOOKS are published by

Kensington Publishing Corp.
850 Third Avenue
New York, NY 10022

All Kensington Titles, Imprints, and Distributed Lines are available at special quantity discounts for bulk purchases for sales promotions, premiums, fund-raising, and educational or institutional use. Special book excerpts or customized printings can also be created to fit specific needs. For details, write or phone the office of the Kensington special sales manager: Kensington Publishing Corp., 850 Third Avenue, New York, NY 10022, attn: Special Sales Department, Phone: 1-800-221-2647.

Pinnacle and the P logo Reg. U.S. Pat. & TM Off.

First Printing: May 2003
10 9 8 7 6 5 4

Printed in the United States of America

ACKNOWLEDGMENTS

Many people helped in the preparation of this book. I would particularly like to thank Michelle Conkle, Aron Miller, Ron Bamieh, and Kevin Drescher. I'd also like to thank my wonderful literary agent, Damaris Rowland, and terrific editor at Pinnacle Books, Michaela Hamilton.

I
SKIN HEAD DOGS

ONE

PLAYING WITH FIRE

Ventura, California

Katrina Montgomery was one of those southern California golden girls. Blessed with good looks, a full head of luxuriant red hair, and a winning personality, she seemed to have everything going for her. She had loving parents, an upper-middle-class home, and lots of friends. Her mother, Katy, recalled, "I had Trina when I was very young, but I was excited about it and immediately fell in love with her. Because my husband and I were so young, we made a decision we would wait a few years before finishing with having our family. So it gave me almost five years to have just Trina. She was very special. She talked in full sentences when she was just two. She had a sense of humor when she was a baby and knew how to make everybody laugh and be silly."

Katrina had many cousins to play with, since her mother's family was so large and lived in the surrounding area. She was gifted, headstrong, and knew how to make her way in the world, even as a child. Her father was a civil litigator, and though the family was not incredibly rich, they did live in a very comfortable environment in an area that was booming.

Katrina Montgomery inhabited a town that was a fabled locale on the southern California coast. With palm trees, soft breezes, and innumerable sunny days, Ventura had an exotic, postcard feel about it. The mission located there, San Buenaventura, was founded in 1782 by Father Junipero Serra. The town grew up amidst an array of vineyards, small farms, and the Pacific Ocean at its doorstep. As Spud Hilton wrote in his travel article for the *San Francisco Chronicle*, "With its historic sites, respected winery, sizeable marina, rabid surf culture, and a past built on earthquakes, orchards, and oil—Ventura is a California collage, a Whitman Sampler of what defines the state . . . a nicely wrapped bundle of Golden State–ness."

But Katrina Montgomery wanted more than just beaches, sunshine, and a Gidget-type lifestyle. She liked to walk on the wild side. Her father, Michael, remembered, "In the sixth and seventh grade at St. Thomas Aquinas School, she was considered the Villanova scholarship candidate. We were told that if she would apply herself and take a couple of extra courses, she had it in the bag. But by that point in her life, she had already started into the era where she thought she was smarter than everyone. I think it fostered a sense of invincibility on her part. By the time she was in ninth grade, she became somewhat rebellious and went through the 'turmoil days,' as I call them, that most teenagers go through. In Trina's case, it came about a little sooner than most. She insisted on transferring from St. Bonaventure High School to Ventura High. It got to a point where we were struggling just to keep her in high school."

While attending Ventura High, Katrina met and befriended Scott Porcho. He could be termed as coming from the "other side of the tracks." Or, this being California, "the other side of the freeway." Scott was a large boy with a rough exterior and rough friends. He could be either a good friend or a dangerous enemy, depending on whether he liked you or not. Porcho was also one of the founders of Ventura's Skin Head Dogs, a skinhead gang with neo-Nazi beliefs, a taste for violent punk rock music, and a penchant for brawling.

As Katrina Montgomery spent time with Scott Porcho and his friends, she began to adopt more and more of their sense of rebelliousness. These ideas, so foreign to typical middle-class life, became further entrenched when she began to date Mitchell Sutton. Sutton, along with Porcho, was one of the founders of the Skin Head Dogs, and his racist beliefs were even more strident than Porcho's. This band of rowdy and often dangerous young men fit right into Katrina's own sense of rebellion. Though she was not an extreme racist herself, she nonetheless hung out with this gang of "skinhead brothers," attracted to the wild life they represented. Even if they were underage, there was nothing she and the others liked better than partying and drinking. And when her boyfriend, Mitch Sutton, decided to join the army and was stationed in Germany, all hell broke loose in the Montgomery household. Katrina insisted on joining him there, even though she was still very young.

Her father recalled, "She was only sixteen. After several months of conflict in our household, at the advice of my younger brother, we decided to stop banging our heads against the wall and let Trina see the real world. In this case it meant letting her go to Europe with her boyfriend, Mitch Sutton. As my brother pointed out, if she gets a chance to see the real world and live in Wiesbaden, Germany, and freeze her tail off during the winter, perhaps she will turn the corner. It was the best advice anyone's ever given me. Within six months, our daughter came back from Germany and truly did turn the corner. Soon thereafter, she went back and got her GED."

Katy Montgomery concurred about the dramatic change

in her daughter. "Once she came home from Germany, it was like before, but even better. She had a renewed appreciation for family and for her dad and me. Just for authority. She realized that she was too big for her britches, and it had humbled her in a way. She had grown up so that when she came home at seventeen, she was far beyond her years. We were able to kind of move on to a girlfriend stage, and I didn't have to be such a mother figure anymore. We got even closer as she was eighteen and nineteen. We spent a lot of time together having coffee, shopping, and sewing."

It wasn't until around the time that her family was getting ready to move from Ventura to Los Angeles in 1990 that Katrina Montgomery began to break her ties with the Skin Head Dogs, and started distancing herself from Mitch Sutton. She took on the job of a waitress and attended classes at Santa Monica City College. It was there that she saw another world beyond the rough gang who inhabited the environs of Ventura Avenue.

Her father recalled, "She enrolled in Santa Monica City College, actively pursuing a career in photography as an undergraduate, and working full time in Jerry's Deli. The sky was the limit as far as where she was gonna go."

Katrina had a real eye for photography and developed a friendship with professional photographer Keith Leatherwood of Santa Barbara. He agreed that she had a talent in this field.

But even with this new perspective, Katrina did not totally sever her ties with the Skin Head Dogs. She was still friends with Scott Porcho and his wife, Apryl Porcho, and in 1990 she began to write letters to a Skin Head Dog member who was a good friend of Scott's named Justin Merriman. Merriman had been a buddy of Scott's for years and had recently been sent to the California Youth Authority for attacking a young man in Ventura County with a baseball bat. Montgomery knew Merriman not only through the Porchos, but because of his association with Mitch Sutton, as well. She had met Merriman at some of the Skin Head Dog parties and thought he was cute. She was also aware that he could be violent, but Montgomery was very headstrong and self-assured, believing that she could handle any situation. As her father had said, Katrina tended to live by her own rules.

It started out innocently enough. Justin Merriman was just another inmate seeking female correspondence from the outside, and Katrina Montgomery was willing to write him back. In a letter sent in January 1990, Merriman wrote, "Trina, I was surprised to hear from you. Well, it looks like I did blow it. A big step from the Hall. All the way to Youth Authority. It's gonna be for awhile. I don't know where I'm going. Hopefully not crazy."

Merriman went on to say that he heard she was in independent studies and he seemed to confuse this with study hall. He said that he had been in there himself and always got into trouble. He constantly argued with the African-American teacher and got thrown out after calling her a "big fat N word," as he put it. But he said it didn't matter since he never did any work in there anyway.

Justin commented that it must be kind of rough on her relationship with Mitch Sutton, since he was still in Germany and she was in southern California. Then he asked how things were going with Apryl Porcho, and that he'd heard that she and Apryl had taken a road trip down the coast. Merriman knew that Apryl Porcho had been jealous of all of Scott's girlfriends and realized that Katrina was one of Scott's closest female friends. But the fact that Scott and Apryl were now married seemed to have allayed any fears Apryl might have had about any romantic inclinations between Scott and Katrina. They were more like good buddies than anything else.

Finally Merriman got down to his real reason for writing. He wanted to be set up with one of Katrina's girlfriends.

> Set the homie up with a firm nina and white. Tell 'em how gentle and caring I am, and how I don't think about sex, not a pervert, and I'll buy 'em anything. He, he, ha, ha!
> Well, I'm sorry for writing like a sloppy bum. Hope you can read it.
> Love, Justin."

Soon thereafter he sent her another letter. He said that whenever he got mail it was like Christmas morning to him. He told her to cut out the gangster writing and symbols in her letters because the staff always watched for those types of things. Then he related that Mitch Sutton never seemed to learn this lesson no matter how many times he told him.

"When I went to Colston the staff would let me read his letters up at the desk. Every time I wrote him back I would say watch what he wrote. And sure enough the next letter would have racial and gang shit in it. But I loved his ass for writing me all the time!"

Merriman noted that both Katrina Montgomery and Mitch Sutton were by now dating other people and that it must be awfully hard on their relationship with such a great distance between them. He nonetheless chided Sutton, who most likely had started taking out other women first. Justin wrote her, "He tells you he's messin around with two German broads. Well that dirty dog male shovenist [*sic*] slob. Is he trying to make you jealous or something?"

Then Merriman couldn't resist adding a bit of his own male "shovenist" bravado. He said, "What I get sick of, I get some winch [*sic*] and train her so she gets used to the rules and all that, but they still act dumb and get cocky."

Then he said for her to send him some photos, and added, "I should be gettin' some taken of [me]. That smooth Peckerwood Mr. Merriman. It's probably best I never went up to Germany. I would probably get drunk and beat up Mitch's German homies. If they're like you tell me I would laugh my ass off! What a bunch of faggots."

By March 1990, Justin Merriman was still polite and civil for the most part in his letters to Katrina, commenting about her recent trip to Hawaii. "Tell me how your trip to the island went. Didn't you go by your lonesome? Those pictures you sent me were good even though you make me send em back! What kind of games you playin' woman? Thanks for lettin' me at least check them out. Let me admire some more. There's not much more to babble about my homely little life, here."

Soon thereafter he became somewhat irritated and accused Katrina of playing games with him for not setting him up with one of her girlfriends. He said, "Tell me what's up with your friends. Give me a damn hookup. I know you got some fine winch [*sic*] in store for me. Knowin' you, you'll play some game."

He told her that those "queer bastards" at her work were going to learn to fear him. He called them "penis eatin' bastards" and flamers, and said they made him sick.

Merriman told her to write him about her troubles since he had plenty of time to think about them. Then he admitted to something that was bothering him. He stated that no one except Katrina was writing to him anymore.

Reminiscing about old times, Merriman wrote in a letter dated June 5, 1990, that he remembered an occasion when they'd both been sitting in a hot tub at one of the Skin Head Dog parties. He wistfully recalled that she had given him a foot rub and how good it felt. "I keep thinking about when Jeff, James, you and I brought like four or five cases and kicked it in that jacuzzi. It seemed like we spent all night getting drunk and junk. Aye, I even got a foot rub type o thing. Hey are you going to give me another one. Every time I drink while spending hours in a jacuzzi I feel nice and fucked up."

He asked her if she'd heard anything about Bridget Callahan. Then asked if she might be able to shoot him a few more photos.

Up until August 1990 Justin Merriman had been in the California Youth Authority. But that month when he turned eighteen they were shipping him off to state prison because he had attacked a guard in the CYA. Instead of being afraid of the change, he said that he welcomed it. It would increase his stature within the Skin Head Dogs. He commented a little about her move to Los Angeles, Mitchell Sutton's removal from the scene, and then he got to his real intentions. "I've been thinking since Mitch kind of called it quits, I could write you obscene type shit. See I was lookin' here at this neat picture you sent and thought I'd ask you if you'd consider letting me play with the toys you must have under that buttercup suit. Would it be yes, no, maybe? Think of something good to tell me."

Her reply is now lost, but she seems not to have been offended by his remarks. Instead by September 27, 1990, he wrote, "I want a picture of you in a G-string."

Merriman was less happy when he learned she was now dating a young man who attended the University of Southern California. And in a fit of peevishness he commented, "Why does everyone get a date with you except me?"

In December 1990, Justin Merriman was placed in Corcoran State Prison, one of the toughest in the state. It was a dangerous and violent place, filled with opposing gang members affiliated with the Arayan Brotherhood, the Mexican Mafia, the Crips, and the Bloods. In fact, it was one of the most dangerous prisons in America. The authorities had reportedly placed inmates with different gang affiliations there so they would fight and could be punished. In effect, they wanted to break the back of the gangs in Corcoran State Prison.

But the place was an absolute zoo. The deputy warden of San Quentin Prison, Lewis Fudge, said of Corcoran in this period, "It was akin to forcing the integration among Catholics and Protestants of Northern Ireland." The fights among prisoners at Corcoran reached to a startling 1,500 during the first year alone. That was nearly one fight per prisoner. Daniel McCarthy, the retired director of the California Department of Corrections, said, "The level of violence was absolutely the highest I have ever seen in any institution anywhere in the country."

Justin Merriman did not go into detail about his dangerous new surroundings to Montgomery. He had other things on his mind, which included having her send him pornographic material. In fact, by the time he got to Corcoran Prison, Merriman's letter affair with Katrina Montgomery began heating up. He told her, "I can be out next year. You won't be lonely long, sugar shorts! I'm shooting on out of here with a quickness with fantasies to be fulfilled. Let me sound like a used car dealer for a minute. I have a deal for you, you can't refuse. I'm the crafty craft master."

Merriman told her she was in a losing relationship with her college boyfriend. She didn't respect him and he understood why. Joe Jock, as Merriman called him, didn't come from the 'hood and he wasn't into white power. How could anyone like Katrina respect a guy like that? he wondered. He derided the fact that her college boyfriend had recently taken her to a professional basketball game. According to Merriman, basketball was only played by "overpaid niggers" and wasn't worth watching.

He told her that she would lose her mind if she kept watching "professional monkeys" play basketball. It would make her despondent enough to want to commit suicide.

Then he added, "All is just about lost when out of nowhere comes a real handsome white man with hair on his barrel chest and a heart of gold. Every woman's dream, every nigger's nightmare. He pulls up drinking Night Train and smoking nonfiltered cigs, looking very manly, like baby-faced Malone [*sic*]. Slick dog written all over him. And he spots her. Yes, she knows deep down this is worth living for, worth killing for!

"He sweeps her off her feet. They fall deeply in love, have kinky sex, make five pure white Nazi low-ride kids, living happily ever after! The end."

Then he told her that if she wanted to, she could write him some smut so that he could pleasure himself.

He signed the letter, "The Mighty Mister Merriman."

By February 26, 1991, the letter relationship was becoming even more torrid. Merriman wrote, "Other inmates are getting jealous of my righteous redhead telephone raping honey buns. I've heard your mouth gets busy when the booze hits the neck. Know what? I dig a mouthy lady. That came from straight from the heart. So is we on like donkey kong? Or are [you] still playing shy girl?"

And of a recent phone sex call he said, "Blew my mind what you did on that phone call. I felt like I was on some erotic true sexual confessions [trip]. Tell you what, it's a straight sin a girl with looks and style as yourself not getting hosed down the way you'd like to get it. I'll probably dream of a nasty red snapper all fucking night long."

By July 14, 1991, Merriman was full of bravado and wrote Montgomery about a guy she was dating that he would have beaten up if he was out of jail: "Dearest Buttercup Baby. He don't have any dibbs on our hina from the mighty Ventura. I've made up my mind, he's got to get his ol slinky snake like self under a rock. And in the process not leave no snail slime."

Once again he asked what she was doing with Joe Jock. The guy wasn't into white power, had no gang ties, and was a complete "lame" in his opinion. He then asked what in hell she was doing dating him. Was she desperate for company?

In fact, Merriman was derogatory in most of his remarks about her college experience. The real life was on the Avenue in Ventura. All the rest was just prissy middle-class crap that didn't add up to anything.

He told her that he was better than Joe Jock and she knew it. He said she couldn't want for better. He claimed he had nice red facial hair, and a Nazi low-ride crop top haircut. Merriman proclaimed that he made the town and the white race look good. Then he added that he could wrestle a "sweaty bug-eyed nigga" around the cell for five minutes and roll his cigarette with spunk and class afterward.

He bragged that he was a perfect specimen of the Anglo-Saxon race. She couldn't want for a better ideal of the Nazi type.

I'll get down to the nitty gritty. I'm so white. So lovingly white! Nothing but pure genetics. Irish and Welsh blood flow through this mighty White. Fuck, I'm of excellent stock of wonderful whiteness. I'm so fucking great! I was born the great white hope. Who knows, you might be lucky enough to bear a few kids from my excellent stock.

He joked that it might cost her though. He said it was hard work creating babies since it put pressure on his nut sack. But he added that they could work out a deal so that he could give her his super baby-making jism. He said it was extra thick for superior babies.

He joked how some girls tried to trick him. Play it like they were begging for excellent babies from him, when in fact all they wanted to do was use him as a sex toy, craving his "secret sauce," as he put it. He joked that it pissed him off to be used for their sick pleasures.

"I'm sure you have good intentions, though," he said. "When I'm shaggin' a white girl down I'm thinking strictly of the race. Now am I down for the cause or what? What a guy."

Ten days later his bravado hadn't diminished. Merriman told her about a photo he sent her: "Look at that massive chest! Big monster-sized hood. I know you want to just touch it. Well, if I'm in the right mood and you ask me in a sweet style, I'll let you touch my barrel chest once. I'm not promising nothing. I hate being used in that manner. I gave up being a sex symbol years ago. But for all you've done for me while I've been down, I'll give you that kind of action."

Then in midsentence he stopped and reported that they'd just had an earthquake. He said it had caught him by surprise, and a cigarette dropped right out of his mouth and into his lap. Merriman hated earthquakes and was truly frightened by them. He said that in 1989 he had been in the Youth Authority when a big quake hit. He told her that he had been kickin' back, smoking and listening to his radio as peaceful as could be, when *bam*, the floor started shaking and the walls started swaying. Toilet water was splashing out of the bowl and the pad was rocking, and he was afraid the whole place would fall in on him. He related that the walls already were full of cracks and the concrete looked like it would come tumbling down at any time, even without the aid of an earthquake. He thought he was a goner for sure. As he put it, "I was already a loser. But then I thought I was gonna be a dead loser. Fuck, I'm too young. But here I am writing Mistress Katrina, my Li'l Red Haired Devil to this day. Oh, and I made it past my nineteenth birthday. By the way Trina, you filled out real healthy from that last time I seen you in a bathing suit in Jeff's pool."

Then he added that he wasn't laying his "Mac" on her just to get her panties down. He admitted he knew more about her from her letters than he did from partying with her in years past. Then he told her to learn how to handle her booze better.

"I've had the run down on your drunkeness. Pretty impressive, I might add, but hopefully that lip doesn't turn on me." Then, he warned her, "It would get ugly, real ugly."

Apparently she had sent him another sexy photo, and he commented at the end of the letter, "It was exciting erection arousing."

Sometime between July 1991 and February 1992, Katrina Montgomery visited Justin Merriman while he was in prison. Her thoughts about these occasions have not survived, but his have. In a letter dated February 11, 1992, he stated, "We're friends forever and since we're honest to goodness friends, I'll be honest and tell you, you looked good at visiting. I was kind of speechless for a few seconds. I would have loved to dry hump you. But I remembered myself not to get weird on you."

Then he closed with a question that began to bother him more and more. "[Are you] Miss Hard to Get?"

Apparently Katrina Montgomery visited him again in late February or early March 1992. On March 4, Merriman commented, "I apologize for my rude and crude sexual gestures while you visited. I walked back to my building with a gang of unused Nazi babies in my pants screaming your name."

He added that he might have overdone the drama at her visit there and she should not fear him. Then he told her about the benefits of having an inmate boyfriend.

But at the end of the letter he commented once again about her hard-to-get attitude. He said he knew she was interested in him but at the same time thought she was better than he was. He was sure he was being used. But he warned her this attitude might come back to haunt her. He added, "All bullshit aside, what are you after??"

The very next day he was even more adamant in questioning her intentions about him.

Trina, I would be more than happy to lend a helping hand with you and [Mitch Sutton]. The whole reason I brought all this up, is why are you doing all this for me? It sure isn't 'cause you want me. You were way out disgusted, sick to your guts with even swapping spit with me. What do you want from me???

He told her that her line about needing a friend didn't cut it anymore. He knew she didn't want him to tell Mitch Sutton that they had been kissing or where she had put her hand on his body. Then he said if she was interested to give him a try. If it was something else, he wanted to know. He was tired of all the waiting on her part and being coy. Merriman added, "Tell me what you are wanting from me."

The letters from Justin Merriman to Katrina Montgomery became more and more strident and accusatory. According to Katrina's friend Shawna Burgess, Katrina stopped writing him about this time because Merriman's letters were becoming "so weird." And then in the early summer of 1992, Justin Merriman was released from prison and back on the streets of Ventura.

According to Shawna Burgess, Justin Merriman's letters

and phone calls to Katrina Montgomery did not cease when he got out of prison. In fact, they became even more strident and sexual in nature. In desperation, Montgomery told him to stop writing and phoning her. She even decided to go to Justin Merriman's residence on Miller Court in Ventura, where he was now living with his mother and sister, to tell him to stop bugging her. In Shawna Burgess's own words, "She had some things to take care of."

What happened next comes in two slightly different versions, one told by Katrina Montgomery to her mother, Katy, and the other to her friend Shawna, whom she'd known since her days in St. Bonaventure High School. In the story to her mother, Katrina related that she'd talked with Justin at his home, and then Justin's mother, Beverlee Sue Merriman, asked if she would like to stay over for the night since it was late and a long drive back to Los Angeles. Katrina agreed and made ready for bed in a guest bedroom. As she lay down on the bed, Justin crept into her room.

Katy Montgomery related later, "She told me she was [awakened] by Justin, who climbed into bed with her and was making sexual advances. He was rubbing himself against her. She tried to say no and he wouldn't listen."

Katrina finally persuaded Justin that she needed to use the bathroom before they went any further. But once he got off of her, she grabbed her belongings and fled out the door.

In Katy Montgomery's version, Katrina jumped into her truck and drove away at a high rate of speed as Justin chased her out the door.

In Shawna Burgess's version the details were somewhat different. Shawna said she was sitting in the vehicle for nearly twenty minutes listening to a tape of Joe Jackson while Katrina was in the Merriman residence. Suddenly Katrina came running out the door. As they drove away, Montgomery told her that Justin had tried to sexually assault her. She said he had been rubbing himself up against her. Burgess recalled, "She was crying and very upset. She had red marks around her neck. She said, 'Justin got mad. He attacked me.'"

Burgess was sure that he had tried to choke her friend. As in the other version, Katrina said she escaped by feigning to use the bathroom.

In both versions Katrina Montgomery revealed a chilling fact. She said Beverlee Sue Merriman walked into the room and witnessed Justin Merriman assaulting her. The woman didn't say a word or do anything to stop her son. Mrs. Merriman simply watched as Justin assaulted Katrina, and then walked away without a word.

TWO

"I'M GOING TO GET THAT BITCH!"

In November 1992, Larry Nicassio was a sixteen-year-old member of a skinhead gang known as the Sylmar Family. Located in the town of Sylmar, Los Angeles County, this city was a northerly suburb of Los Angeles and about fifty miles from Ventura down Highway 118. Nicassio had been a member of the gang since he was twelve years old. Known as "Little Larry" for his size and age, Nicassio was the youngest member of the gang, which was made up mainly of his brothers, cousins, and close friends.

Two of Nicassio's cousins, Ryan Bush and Robert Bush, were also members of the Sylmar Family. Nicassio had spent a great deal of time with them since childhood and had bounced around homes, alternately living with his father and grandparents. One of Larry's main reasons for being in the gang was his admiration of eighteen-year-old Ryan Bush and especially twenty-year-old Robert Bush. In fact, by 1992 Larry Nicassio was living in the Bushes' home. The Sylmar Family had in effect become his family.

The Sylmar Family had close ties with the Skin Head Dogs in Ventura and espoused the same beliefs of white supremacy and neo-Nazi rhetoric. Like the Skin Head Dogs, members of the "Family" wore Nazi tattoos and had even defaced the exterior of a local Jewish synagogue with Nazi slogans and swastikas. And like the Skin Head Dogs, the Sylmar Family members loved to drink, party, and fight.

Larry Nicassio knew Scott Porcho and realized that the Skin Head Dogs were in some regards even more violent than the Sylmar Family. Porcho was a good fighter and could stomp an opponent down within seconds. The way the Skin Head Dogs achieved status was by attacking people of color, breaking the law, and moving upward in the judicial and prison systems. Everything that stood as a symbol of "outlaw" was desirable in their eyes.

Nicassio also knew Katrina Montgomery, having seen her at several skinhead parties in Ventura and in Oxnard, where Scott Porcho and his wife, Apryl, owned a home. Nicassio knew that Katrina wasn't a hard-core Skin Head Dog girl, but someone on the edge of the gang. She had been dating Mitchell Sutton, but wasn't averse to going out on her own, as well. Nicassio had even been in a car with her and others on a trip to Mexico. And although he thought she was an attractive girl, Nicassio knew that he was much too young for her to take any interest in him. Four years' difference can mean a lot when you're sixteen and twenty years old, respectively. They exchanged pleasantries at parties and nothing more.

One of the things Larry Nicassio observed while at parties was that Katrina Montgomery could not hold her liquor. Normally vivacious and bright, when drinking she became loud, rambunctious, and often combative. Especially verbally. At such times, according to him, she lived up to the reputation of a "fiery redhead."

One other person in this orbit that Larry Nicassio admired and feared was Justin Merriman. Merriman had a nasty reputation as a fighter and was considered one of the toughest gang members of the Skin Head Dogs. Nicassio had even witnessed Merriman beat an opponent senseless during a fight. To Nicassio, Merriman was the embodiment of everything a skinhead ought to be: race-pure, tough, and afraid of no one.

On November 27, 1992, after a Thanksgiving dinner, Larry Nicassio, Ryan Bush, and several other Sylmar Family members went to a party at Scott Porcho's house in Oxnard. When Nicassio arrived, he noticed that Katrina Montgomery was already there and seemed to be drunk. She had attended her family's traditional Thanksgiving dinner in Los Angeles, with the usual holiday fare. Then she had driven her blue Toyota pickup truck to Porcho's home, after lying to her parents that she was going to visit a friend in Santa Barbara, and then would go over to her grandparents' house. Katrina knew that her parents did not approve of her skinhead friends. Mrs. Montgomery was already afraid for her because of the incident at Justin Merriman's home, where he had assaulted her. Mrs. Montgomery wanted Katrina to stay away from all the Skin Head Dogs.

While at the party, Nicassio noticed that Katrina Montgomery and Justin Merriman would talk for a while and then separate. It was hard to figure out what was going on. One moment they seemed like a girlfriend and boyfriend, and then they were very distant. As the evening progressed, Nicassio could see that Merriman was becoming very upset with Montgomery. Whenever she tried to "kiss and make up," he would push her away. According to both Nicassio and Bush, it was a rowdy party with alcohol being consumed pretty freely, as well as meth and even LSD.

Scott Porcho knew that trouble was brewing. Even before the party began he had told Justin that Katrina Montgomery would be coming. Merriman responded by saying, "Well, just keep her away from me." Porcho knew that Merriman had taken it very hard when Montgomery refused to answer his letters or phone calls after he had been released from prison. Porcho said later, "Because of all the letters she sent him in prison, Justin thought she would be his girlfriend when he got out. But she didn't want anything to do with him when he got out. It pissed him off."

In fact, Merriman was even more "pissed off" now because of the recent incident when he had wanted sex with her and she escaped by feigning to go to the bathroom and running out the door. But Porcho's house was too small for Merriman and Montgomery to be separated for long, and as the evening progressed, Katrina became more and more drunk, and in Merriman's words, "mouthy." A couple of nasty incidents happened that several people would remember later. At one point, Merriman pinned Katrina Montgomery down on a bed with his body. At first she giggled, but then she started screaming for him to get off of her. Scott Porcho rushed into the room to find Montgomery crying and several skinheads standing around her menacingly. She was holding her stomach as if someone had just punched her there.

While Apryl Porcho escorted Katrina out of the room, Scott asked what had happened. Merriman told him, "Nothin' happened."

"You sure?" Porcho asked.

"Yeah, I'm sure," Merriman responded.

Porcho cleared the room of all the skinheads, including Merriman.

After this incident, Merriman told Ryan Bush, "I'm going to get that bitch!" And he told Larry Nicassio several times, "We're gonna get her."

Merriman started passing Nicassio steak knives from the kitchen, and said, "Get her."

Nicassio thought it was a joke, and at one point he stood behind Montgomery, aiming the steak knife at her head and making the noises used in the film *Psycho* while pantomiming stabbing her in the head.

Around 3:00 A.M. things were escalating. Justin Merriman backed Katrina Montgomery up against a wall, threatening her while Nicassio and Ryan Bush stood nearby. On Merriman's instructions, Nicassio moved in on Katrina and began to choke her. One of the guests, John Cundiff, just happened to look up from the dining room table and witnessed this. He told Scott Porcho, "Look," and pointed toward Nicassio and Montgomery. It took only moments for Scott Porcho to fly into a rage. He ran toward Katrina, pushed Nicassio out of the way, knocked Ryan Bush down, kicked him in the ribs, and smashed a beer bottle into Merriman's forehead.

Katrina slapped Larry Nicassio in the face and yelled, "You can't touch me, I'm property of the Skin Head Dogs!"

Meanwhile, a rampant Scott Porcho and bleeding Justin Merriman fought around the room, knocking over items and swinging like madmen. Neither one of them gave an inch, even though Merriman was bleeding profusely. Porcho gave Merriman credit; he said later that Justin would not give up.

Porcho recounted, "[Justin] had a piece of glass sticking out of his head. But he fought well."

The wild brawl went on until they nearly knocked over a large fish tank, which by some reports contained a snake. This brought an end to the fight.

As soon as it was over, Katrina went into the bathroom with Merriman to help him clean his wound. This thoroughly confused Ryan Bush. One moment Merriman and Montgomery were fighting like cats and dogs and the next moment they seemed to have kissed and made up. Not much of anything was making sense to Bush in the Porcho home that evening.

Things got even stranger when Apryl Porcho returned home after giving a ride to a partygoer. She saw all the blood and mess on the floor and screamed at everyone to clean it up. For some reason, the tough guys complied. Apryl then told Justin Merriman, Ryan Bush, and Larry Nicassio she would drive them to Merriman's house, since their rides had already left. Much of her reasoning was just to get them out of the house before anything else happened. As they drove down the street, Apryl Porcho looked over and noticed that Merriman's forehead had stopped bleeding. Her observation would become important later.

Apryl Porcho returned home after about an hour to find a still drunk and unstable Katrina Montgomery. By now, Katrina was insisting that she go over to Justin Merriman's house. She had received a phone call from him while Apryl was on the road home and he asked her to come over. Apryl repeatedly tried talking her out of it. She knew just how angry Merriman was with Katrina, despite what he might have told her over the phone. But Montgomery was so insistent that they soon began arguing over the subject.

"You don't tell me how to run my life!" Katrina said.

"I want you to stay," Apryl responded. "I haven't seen you in a long time."

Katrina insisted on going. Nothing Apryl did or said could dissuade Katrina from leaving. Finally, out of tiredness and frustration, Apryl threw Katrina her truck keys and told her to leave. She watched Katrina Montgomery get into her blue pickup truck and drive away.

Nicassio, Bush, and Merriman had arrived at Justin's home somewhere between 3:00 and 4:30 on the morning of

November 28, 1992. They ate some bagels in the kitchen and then retired to Justin's room. His bedroom was located over the garage, and could be entered only by climbing some stairs within the residence and then leaving the main house and crossing a small footbridge. Once inside the bedroom, Justin gave Nicassio and Bush some sleeping bags and blankets so they could sleep on the floor. Nicassio was given an old pink electric blanket to add to his sleeping bag.

While Larry Nicassio laid out his bedding, he heard Merriman in a phone conversation with someone. As soon as the conversation was over, Merriman turned to him and said that Katrina Montgomery was coming over to the house. Once again, this made little sense to Nicassio, since he knew how angry Merriman had been with Montgomery only a short time earlier. Ryan Bush was surprised, as well. Merriman and Montgomery had been arguing so much at Scott Porcho's house that he was sure he never wanted to see her again.

A short time later Katrina Montgomery arrived, sometime around 5:00 A.M., carrying a black overnight bag and wearing a white T-shirt, blue jean overalls, and white tennis shoes. She left the room for a few minutes, and when she returned she was wearing her "sleeping clothes," which consisted of a sweatshirt and sweatpants. She crawled into bed with Justin as Nicassio and Bush lay on the floor.

What happened next became indelibly etched into both Larry Nicassio's, and Ryan Bush's minds, although they remembered slightly different details of the events that transpired. Nicassio heard Merriman and Montgomery talking and then arguing in bed. He looked up to see Merriman straddle Montgomery's body with his own. Merriman pulled down his underwear and told her to orally copulate him. "No," she said, "not with [Nicassio and Bush] in here." Merriman slapped her. "Shut up and do it!" he demanded.

Most likely out of fear, she began to comply with his wishes. Sixteen-year-old Larry Nicassio was in complete shock. Only inches from his head, Katrina Montgomery was giving Justin Merriman "a blow job," as he put it. Out of embarrassment and fear, Nicassio pretended to be asleep. But he was far from asleep. He watched as Merriman disrobed Katrina and began to have vaginal sex with her. She resisted and said, "I don't want to become pregnant."

But Merriman forced himself on her, and as he ejaculated he said, "There, now you're pregnant."

It didn't stop there. For the next two hours Merriman forced Katrina Montgomery into various sexual acts. All the while Katrina was begging him to stop. She said it hurt. Both Nicassio and Bush were too afraid of Merriman to intervene. Merriman even forced Montgomery down on the side of the bed near Nicassio, better to orally copulate him. She continued to ask him to stop, but he totally ignored her pleas.

"My mouth hurts!" she cried. "Please, let me go to the bathroom."

Merriman's reply was, "No. You can do it in the waste-basket!"

At this point Merriman asked Nicassio and Bush if they wanted part of the action. They both declined. But Bush did speak up and say, "Let her go to the bathroom."

Merriman growled at Bush, "Shut up! If I let her go to the bathroom, she'll sneak out and tell on us."

Katrina Montgomery rose and sat on the edge of the bed, crying, while she pulled on her panties, sweatpants, T-shirt, and shoes. Larry Nicassio moved a little to the side to give her more room. As he did, he saw an object in Merriman's hand. Bush even heard Montgomery say, "What are you doing, Justin?" just before Merriman plunged a knife into her neck.

She screamed and fell to the floor, begging for her life.

"I can't do it," Merriman replied. "You'll tell the police what I did."

Katrina swore she wouldn't go to the police and kept pleading with him to spare her life.

Larry Nicassio said to Bush, "Let's get out of here!" and began to rise.

Merriman rushed to the door, knife in hand, and yelled, "Shut the fuck up! You'd better shut the fuck up, Larry!"

Merriman turned to Ryan Bush and said, "You better tell your cousin to get right or I'm gonna fucking get him, too!"

Merriman then went back and grabbed bleeding Katrina Montgomery and called her a stupid bitch. He told her to lie down on the floor and covered her with a blanket. Katrina was crying, sobbing and pleading, but did as he said.

Bush tried to speak up, and said to Merriman, "Kick back, dawg. Think about what you're doing!"

Nicassio was in such shock from the violent scene that he put his hands over his ears to shut out Katrina's cries and pleas. He said later that he stared out the window, afraid of what would happen next.

Justin Merriman ignored everyone. He went to his dresser drawers and began to paw through them for something, coming back to Montgomery with a large crescent wrench in his hand. As she lay on the floor moaning, the blanket over her, he hit her as hard as he could in the head with the wrench. The moaning stopped and she crumpled to the floor, unconscious.

Merriman attempted to hand the wrench to Ryan Bush so he could strike her, too. But Bush refused.

"You motherfucker!" Merriman yelled, and threw the wrench down, disgusted with Bush's timidity.

Nicassio by now was nearly crying himself. He stared out the window as hard as he could and heard Merriman say, "Where's the jugular?" Nicassio turned in time to see Merriman holding the knife once again. Merriman pulled on Katrina Montgomery's hair, exposing her neck, and sliced where he thought her jugular vein was. Nicassio jerked his head away again but heard a strange gurgling sound emanating from Katrina Montgomery's throat. The next thing he knew, blood was oozing onto the floor and the blanket where he lay. He scooted away in horror.

But according to Ryan Bush, who saw the whole episode, Nicassio watched as Justin Merriman slashed a fatal knife wound in Katrina Montgomery's neck. Like Nicassio, Bush was stunned speechless by the horrifying turn of events.

Justin Merriman grabbed more blankets and threw them over Katrina Montgomery's now dead body. "Fuck, man," he said to Bush and Nicassio, "do you know what they do to people in prison for rape? We'll all be killed if we go to prison. You're both involved now and you'd better help me get rid of her body."

THREE

SUNSET FARMS

By the time Katrina Montgomery's body lay in a blood-soaked heap on the floor, Ryan Bush and Larry Nicassio were totally freaked out. They desperately wanted to leave the room, but Justin Merriman still threatened them with the knife and told them they weren't going anywhere. He said they were just as much involved in the murder now as he was.

Merriman put the bloody knife and wrench in a plastic bag. Then, as a bit of deception, he phoned Scott Porcho with a potential alibi. He asked Porcho where Katrina Montgomery was and why she had never shown up at his house. Once the phone call was over he told Nicassio to get Katrina Montgomery's pickup truck and bring it closer to the house. Nicassio was so afraid of Merriman that he did as instructed. It was between 8:00 A.M. and 9:00 A.M. now, and the sun was coming up through the haze along the coast. Luckily for Nicassio there were few people up and out on the street at that time.

Meanwhile, Merriman and Bush wrapped Katrina Montgomery's body in the pink electric blanket and carried her across the small footbridge. This took them right past Beverlee Sue Merriman's bedroom window. To Ryan Bush's horror, Mrs. Merriman peeked out the window just as they passed her bedroom. He gasped in a hushed tone, but did not say a word. He continued hauling Montgomery's corpse over the bridge and down the stairs. Neither Merriman nor Bush realized as they descended the staircase that blood oozed out from the blanket and covered various stairs.

They descended the stairs into the living room and went out the front door. Nicassio was waiting in Katrina Montgomery's blue pickup in front of the house, and Merriman and Bush placed Montgomery's body in the truck bed and hopped in the cab. In a state of panic, Bush turned toward Merriman and said, "I can't believe your mother saw us."

But Merriman knew his mother well. He replied, "Don't worry. She'll be cool."

Merriman told Nicassio to drive since he couldn't operate a stick shift. As they pulled away from the curb, they had no idea where they were going other than the fact that they had to dump Montgomery's body somewhere far away from the house. A few options were discussed and then dismissed as being too visible. Still in a state of panic, Ryan Bush said that they should drive to Sylmar and try to get rid of her there. Merriman agreed and they started on the nearly fifty-mile ride toward Sylmar with Montgomery's body in the back of the pickup.

As Nicassio drove on Highway 118, Merriman told him to keep the speed down and not make any sudden lane changes. On the way there, Merriman dug through Montgomery's purse and pulled out some money for gasoline. They drove to Nicassio and Bush's residence on Carlsbad Street in Sylmar, and Bush went inside while Nicassio and Merriman sat in the pickup truck along with Montgomery's body. Ryan woke up Wayne Gibson, who had also been at Porcho's party the night before and was still groggy. Bush asked Gibson for the keys to his truck. Gibson was grouchy about this but gave him the keys and told him to bring it back as soon as he could, since he wanted to use it later. Bush went to the garage, picked up a can of paint thinner, and placed it in the back of Gibson's pickup truck. Then he told Nicassio and Merriman to follow from him.

With Bush in one pickup and Nicassio and Merriman in the other, they drove all over Sylmar trying to find a location to dump Katrina Montgomery's body. But it was midmorning by now and there were people at every location they chose. In frustration, Bush drove to a locale north of Sylmar known as Sunset Farms. It was in a rural area and used by picnickers and hikers. Luckily for them it was deserted now.

Bush had Nicassio follow him up an isolated back road to a bend in the low hills. Determining that no one was nearby, Bush and Merriman pulled Katrina Montgomery's body out of the back of the pickup while Nicassio stood guard. They headed down a ravine next to the road and placed her body in a large steel drainage pipe. They shoved it far enough back in the pipe so that it could not be seen from the road. When they climbed back out of the ravine, they were certain no one had seen them.

It was now time to get rid of Katrina Montgomery's pickup. Ryan Bush had Nicassio and Merriman follow him up into the Angels Crest area of the nearby national forest to a location known as Little Tujunga Canyon. They all stepped out at an isolated spot and proceeded to wipe down Montgomery's pickup with paint thinner to remove bloodstains and fingerprints. Once this was done, Bush attempted to push Montgomery's truck down over a steep embankment, using Gibson's truck as a battering ram. But Montgomery's pickup became entangled in the underbrush and wouldn't budge. It was lodged at a forty-five-degree angle and clearly visible from the road. Afraid that someone would see them if they stayed around any longer, the trio decided to leave it as it was, and departed from the area.

It was afternoon by the time they all got back to Justin Merriman's home in Ventura. He told them, "Make sure Katrina's body is never found." By this he meant they were to go back at some point to Sunset Farms and actually bury her body. He then gave Bush the plastic bag that contained the bloody knife and wrench and told him to get rid of it. Bush said that he would. As Bush and Nicassio headed back to Sylmar, they stopped in an industrial area and Bush threw the plastic bag into a Dumpster.

At this point Bush noticed that he had several bloodstains on his pants. They stopped by an army surplus store and Bush bought a new pair of pants with money he had stolen from Katrina Montgomery's purse, and discarded the blood-stained ones.

Meanwhile, Justin Merriman, back at his house, discovered that his mother and his sister, Ember, had cleaned up the bloodstains left on the stairs. There was a bucket and brush sitting in the house. As Beverlee Sue told Justin later, "I used it to clean up the mess."

While Merriman, Nicassio, and Bush were discarding Montgomery's body and pickup truck, Scott Porcho had a bad feeling about the early morning phone call he had received from Justin Merriman. There was something about it that just didn't ring true. Sometime that afternoon he had Apryl phone Katrina's mother, Katy, and ask if Katrina was there.

Katy Montgomery was surprised by the call from Porcho. She thought Katrina had ceased all contact with the Skin Head Dogs. Katy told Apryl that she thought Katrina was visiting a friend in Santa Barbara. She then asked Apryl if she wanted to leave a message for Katrina, but Apryl answered, "No, I just wanted to tell her something."

Katy Montgomery was unnerved by this phone call. She thought that Katrina Montgomery had broken all ties with the Porchos. In her own words she said, "Katrina had left those Ventura friends behind and was now family-oriented."

Disturbed by this phone call from Apryl Porcho, Katy Montgomery called an acquaintance of Katrina's named Smith. Montgomery wondered if Smith knew where Katrina was. Katy Montgomery was under the impression that her daughter had gone to Santa Barbara to visit a friend, probably Keith Leatherwood. Then Katy explained that she had just received a phone call from Apryl Porcho.

Smith told Katy Montgomery, "Maybe you ought to call Justin Merriman."

This news really struck alarm bells for Katy Montgomery. She knew all about Justin Merriman's previous attack upon her daughter at his residence.

A short time later, Katy Montgomery's fears went into high gear when she received a phone call from the Los Angeles Sheriff's Department. They told her that Katrina Montgomery's blue pickup truck had been found abandoned at Angels Crest in the national forest and Katrina was nowhere in sight. They asked if she knew anything about it. Katy Montgomery was totally mystified as to why her daughter's pickup would be there. Santa Barbara was nearly sixty miles away from that location. There was no plausible reason why Katrina should have driven up to Angels Crest.

Another busy person that day was Beverlee Sue Merriman. According to Justin's sister, Ember, Beverlee Sue had enlisted her aid in cleaning blood off the stairs. When Ember asked where the blood came from, Beverlee Sue explained that it came from Justin. He had been injured at a party the night before. But Ember was somewhat skeptical about this story. Justin had returned home bloody from fights before and there had been no fuss made about it. It seemed as if there was too much urgency in cleaning up this particular blood.

By now phone calls were emanating in all directions concerning the disappearance of Katrina Montgomery. Mike Wozney, a Skin Head Dog member who was a good friend of Justin Merriman, phoned the Merriman residence asking if Larry Nicassio and Ryan Bush needed a ride back to Sylmar. Ember Merriman, Justin's sister, took the call and told Wozney that they were all gone. Then, in a worried tone, she asked, "What's going on?"

Wozney didn't know what she meant by "what was going on." But the tone of her voice worried him.

Ember Merriman wasn't the only one wondering what was going on. At 7:00 P.M. on November 28, Scott Porcho phoned Katy Montgomery and asked if Katrina had made it home. Katy answered no and told him that the sheriff's department had found her abandoned pickup at Angels Crest. Then she asked Porcho if he'd seen Katrina in the last few days. Worried by this latest development, he lied and said that he hadn't. Katy asked if he could give her the phone numbers of Katrina's old skinhead friends in Ventura and Oxnard. But he lied again and said that he didn't have them.

This latest information about Katrina Montgomery's pickup truck being found at Angels Crest only fueled Scott Porcho's suspicions about her disappearance. He phoned Mike Wozney and told him about the fight that had occurred the night before between himself and Merriman, Nicassio, and Bush over Montgomery, when Nicassio had tried choking her. Then he told Wozney, "I think those guys killed her."

When he finished his phone call with Wozney, Scott Porcho instructed Apryl to throw out every steak knife in the house. He got on the phone again and called various Skin Head Dog members, telling them to say there had not been a fight the previous night about Katrina Montgomery, and that she had not been at the party. He told them if they were ever asked about the fight they were to say it was over a card game and accusations of cheating. That was to be the reason he and Justin had started the fight, and why he'd smashed a beer bottle into Justin's head.

Katy Montgomery was busy on the phone, as well, in what would become a marathon session all night long. She had her other daughter, Laurie, keep a diary of when the phone calls were made and to whom.

At 7:30 P.M., Katy phoned the Porcho residence and spoke with Apryl, asking when the last time was she had seen Katrina. Apryl lied and said that it had been months since she'd seen her.

Katy Montgomery next phoned Keith Leatherwood, Katrina's friend in Santa Barbara, and reputedly the person she was going to visit. Leatherwood told Katy that Katrina had phoned him on the night of November 27 and said she was going to a party at the Porcho residence.

At 9:40 P.M., Katy Montgomery phoned Apryl Porcho once more and told her about her conversation with Leatherwood. She asked if Katrina had agreed to come to her party. Apryl Porcho lied again and said that Katrina was supposed to have come by the party but never made it.

At 10:40 P.M., Mike Montgomery, Katrina's father, called Justin Merriman's house. Beverlee Sue Merriman answered the phone. Mike Montgomery asked to speak with Justin, and Beverlee Sue said that he was sleeping, but that she would wake him and have him call Montgomery back.

When there was no reply, Katy Montgomery's sister, Barbara Barnes, phoned the Merriman residence again at 12:30

A.M. on November 29 and got Beverlee Sue Merriman on the line. Barnes said that it had been two hours since Justin had promised to call back and that the Montgomerys were scared. Beverlee Sue answered that she was sorry, but she had fallen asleep and she would get Justin on the line now.

As Justin Merriman came to the phone, Barnes passed the receiver to Katy Montgomery, who asked him if he had seen Katrina. Justin said that he'd last seen Katrina at Scott Porchos house the night before, contradicting the story that the Porchos had been telling her. Now at least Katy Montgomery knew that someone was lying. She attempted to ask Justin some more questions but he clammed up and refused to answer. The next voice Katy Montgomery heard was that of Beverlee Sue Merriman, who said that Justin was sick and that she'd just given him some pills for a fever. He was going back to bed.

At 2:29 A.M. Katy Montgomery phoned the Porcho residence once again and Scott answered the phone. Katy asked to speak with Apryl, and after a short pause she came on the line. Katy said that someone she had just talked to placed Katrina Montgomery at their party of the previous night. Apryl wanted to know who this person was but Katy answered that didn't matter. All she wanted was the truth. There was a long silence, finally broken by Apryl Porcho, who said, "Give me a few minutes."

Montgomery yelled back, "Just tell me if she was there!"

Porcho finally admitted, "Trina was here last night."

"Why did you lie to me, Apryl?" Katy Montgomery demanded.

" 'Cause I was afraid. We didn't want you to think we did something bad to her. We were scared to say we seen her."

"Was Justin Merriman there with her?" Katy asked.

"Yes," Apryl replied. "And they had a pretty good talk. Trina left here at about four A.M."

Apryl then explained that Katrina had left after she had taken Justin Merriman home. She said that she and Katrina had argued about her going over there, and then added that Katrina was not drunk at the time, just upset. Katrina had left the house in her blue pickup and that was the last she'd seen of her.

A day later, after all the worried phone calls by the Montgomerys, on the evening of November 30, 1992, Larry Nicassio and Ryan Bush returned to the Sunset Farms area to bury Katrina Montgomery's body. They took it out of the drainage pipe, and while Nicassio stood guard Bush dug a shallow grave and buried her body. It wasn't a very deep grave, but Bush made sure that it was deep enough so that no scavenging animal would dig it up.

No one had seen them, and Larry Nicassio, Ryan Bush, and Justin Merriman all hoped that their secret would lie buried with her. But in reality their secret was just beginning to become unraveled, even though it would take a long, long time for all the details to come to light.

FOUR

MUMBLES

There was nothing in Justin Merriman's early childhood to presage that he would become a cold-blooded killer. Born on July 22, 1972, to Carson Robison and Beverlee Sue Robison, his given name was Carson Justin Robison. They lived in the small community of Nyland Acres in California's Imperial Valley, less than fifty miles from the Mexican border. The Imperial Valley is a rich farmland surrounded by desert and crisscrossed by irrigation ditches. Its green heartland of tomatoes, cotton, beets, and lettuce is one of the richest farm areas in the world.

Carson Robison worked at raising livestock on their small ranch and making extra money by doing odd jobs and fixing fences. His work often took him away from the homestead. A daughter was born to the Robisons a few years after Justin, and she was named Ember.

The Robison family situation was not always a happy one. Married on New Year's Day, 1970, in Las Vegas, Nevada, Carson and Beverlee Sue often got into arguments as their marriage progressed. In court papers filed later, she stated that during one particularly violent argument, he loaded a shotgun and pointed it at her and the children, swearing that he would kill them and her parents as well.

Beverlee Sue called the police and they came and confiscated Carson's guns. Beverlee Sue later would also claim that he was an alcoholic, while he claimed she had a hair-trigger temper.

One person who became familiar with Justin Merriman's early life was *Ventura County Star* reporter Aron Miller. He conducted an interview with Carson Robison years later, and Robison spoke of his relationship with his son. "[Justin] rode horseback with me on our small Nyland Acres farm and loved to play with the chickens, rabbits, and cows. He was a great kid. Pretty sharp. He liked anything I did, so I took him around with me."

Carson allowed Justin to come along with him as he did odd jobs, and the boy seemed very appreciative of his father's company. But despite Carson and his son's amicable relationship, the situation with his wife was becoming ever more contentious. The arguments increased in scope and frequency, and in March 1973 they separated. By 1974, Beverlee Sue filed a restraining order against Carson, accusing him of trying to sell their livestock and other assets without her permission.

According to Aron Miller, Robison still saw his son and daughter whenever he got a chance. But these visits came to a halt when Beverlee Sue married a man named Dean Merriman. Robison told Miller, "I tried to be around [Justin] occasionally. But then after she married that Merriman, it became a problem for me to go see him."

Beverlee Sue and Dean Merriman married on October 20, 1979, also in Las Vegas, and the family went to live in Casitas Springs, California, just north of Ventura. Situated on the winding Ventura River amidst hills and orange groves with the blue Pacific just down the hill, it was a picture postcard of the fabled southern California landscape. Oil rigs stuck up through the citrus groves like towering sentinels and the fragrant smell of orange blossoms was everywhere. The sun shone most days of the year, and the close proximity of the ocean kept the temperatures from ever getting too hot, even in summer. While snows might cover the peaks of the distant mountains north of town, the winters down in the valley were never cold.

The new marriage and surroundings seemed beneficial to young Carson Justin Robison, who officially changed his name to Justin James Merriman. According to Aron Miller's research, Justin received encouraging marks from his fourth-grade teacher, Mrs. Sherrell, who wrote, "Justin has shown remarkable academic growth and matured socially. I've enjoyed him. Have a good summer."

Justin received mostly B's and C's that year. He did garner an A in handwriting. In citizenship and responsibility he received a C.

The era of marital bliss was not, however, of long duration in the Merriman household. Arguments between Dean and Beverlee Sue became more frequent, and Justin was becoming a troublesome child. According to Tamara Green, a local attorney and friend of Beverlee Sue's, "Justin hung out with the neighborhood kids and would often go to a house down the street where a biker and his girlfriend lived. The biker's girlfriend often gave the children speed and other drugs, and performed sexual favors for them. Justin came to his mother when he was ten and said, 'Mom, I'm taking these pills and I can't stop.' "

Tamara Green went on to say that by the time Justin was eleven, the Merriman household was in a real uproar. In 1982, Dean Merriman filed for divorce, accusing his wife of taking $57,000 from his business, Merriman Grading and Paving Company. But in 1983 he withdrew the papers and they stayed together.

The Merrimans tried to make a go of it from 1985 through

1987, attending scores of counseling sessions, often with Justin in attendance. By now he had very troubling discipline problems. According to documents revealed later in court, the counselor, Thomas Prinz, said he "was trying to help Justin with anger and develop a healthier relationship with his parents." Prinz also warned that without help Justin was in danger of getting himself into trouble with the law. He noted that Justin had a lot of anger boiling just beneath the surface.

Justin did not get along with his stepfather, and in response turned more and more toward his mother. In fact, he began to idolize her. It went way beyond the normal mother/son relationship. He almost seemed to worship her at times. It was a great contradiction. Justin was very polite in his attentions to his mother, but could be like a wild animal around other people and very disrespectful of girls and young women. As far as he was concerned, girls' main purpose in life was to sexually satisfy him.

In 1987, Beverlee Sue Merriman filed for divorce and sought a restraining order against her husband, Dean. In almost a mirror image of her accusations against Carson Robison , she claimed Dean Merriman became "increasingly irrational and angry." She said, "He threatened to kill the family, telling us 'it would be easier if I just eliminated all of you.' He said he would burn down the house and bulldoze the belongings."

In June 1988, when Justin was sixteen, he had his first scrape with the law. He was already hanging out with the Skin Head Dogs and attending their parties. He was also adopting their racist beliefs. In that year he threw a rock through the window of a Jewish temple, and was caught and arrested. According to one source, Justin was unlucky enough to get caught because his fingerprints had been found on one of the rocks. He spent some time in juvenile hall for this incident and apparently lost none of his combativeness or hatred for "Jews and niggers." He fought with other boys there and argued with the counselors.

Slowly but surely, Justin Merriman was absorbing the white supremacist beliefs of the Skin Head Dogs, especially as espoused by Scott Porcho, Mitchell Sutton, and David Ziesmer. Justin's probation officer noticed the lack of parental control being exercised by Beverlee Sue Merriman and recommended that Justin go live with his stepfather. Even Tamara Green noticed this lack of supervision by Beverlee Sue Merriman. She told Aron Miller, "Justin continued his bad behavior and his mother continued to focus on any positives. This was a woman raised on Scarlett O'Hara. When Justin would get into trouble, every day was a new day. Tomorrow we'll begin again."

The probation officer's recommendation that Justin move in with his stepfather went unheeded. By now Justin was enthralled by his mother and had no intentions of being with his stepdad. He would claim later that he hated his stepfather and that the man often beat him. Justin went so far as to have his mother's name tattooed on the back of his neck.

By 1989, the arguments between Beverlee Sue and Dean Merriman had evolved into actual violence. According to Dean Merriman, "She pulled my hair, scratched my face, bit my shoulder, and kicked me in the groin." Beverlee Sue countered that their relationship was absolutely "toxic" and that he was a violent alcoholic. None of this helped Justin Merriman's already volatile nature.

Seething with anger, hating people of different colors and religions, Justin Merriman sought brotherhood and solace in the Skin Head Dogs. Because of his tendency to mumble while speaking, he took on the street gang name of Mumbles. He was a big teenager now, who loved to drink, take drugs, and fight. He gained a reputation as a tough fighter. He was also known as a boy who would slap girls around and abuse them. His anger seemed to spread out in all directions. He hated authority, he hated discipline, and he especially hated "kikes, niggers, and commies."

What Merriman did like was partying with his "brothers" in the gang. It was at one of these parties that he met Katrina Montgomery for the first time. She was not the main attraction for him there. He knew other girls, and she was still young and less well endowed than they were. He seemed to like girls with large breasts, or "big tits," as he put it. He would write later in a derogatory manner about one girl he slept with: "All she had was mosquito bites [for breasts]," he said.

Katrina Montgomery was on the periphary of the girls he knew. But one event did stick in Merriman's memory when it came to her. It was the incident in the hot tub where she rubbed his feet. It was an image of womanhood he desired—a woman who would take care of his needs and desires. He even likened himself to a young lion, and a girlfriend he had later reported that it was up to females to take care of him. In fact, Justin never held down a steady job, and it was always some woman or girl who supported him. More often than not, that woman was his mother.

By 1989, Justin James Merriman was a drinking, drug-taking, fighting time bomb inhabiting the streets of Ventura. But all that was about to change, and before long he would see the inside of the California Youth Authority. On July 3, 1989, at 6:10 P.M., Justin Merriman and a friend named Jeff Ashby drove to Carla Ellison's house in the nearby town of Ojai. Ellison was dating her neighbor, Scott Davis, but Ashby also was interested in her.

When Merriman and Ashby arrived at the Ellison residence, Scott Davis went over to see what was going on. He and Jeff Ashby soon got into a verbal argument about Carla. It got so heated that Carla Ellison ran next door to get Mrs.

Davis. As soon as Patricia Davis arrived on the scene, Justin Merriman grabbed a club out of Ashby's van and pushed it into Scott Davis's face, between his nose and upper lip. Then he told Davis, "You're causing my friend pain. And when my friend is in pain, I'm in pain. And the only way I can relieve my pain is to beat the crap out of you."

He then told Davis, "Get your fucking mother out of here."

Merriman demanded that Mrs. Davis go get Carla Ellison, who was hiding in her house. "Or else!" he said. "I'm getting very agitated."

Mrs. Davis eventually talked Justin Merriman into lowering the club. She said that she and Scott would go into their house and bring Carla Ellison back. Instead, all three of them left and went to her husband's office, where they contacted the police.

Later Patricia Davis would say about Merriman, "I thought he was strung out or something. His eyes were glazed over and he was acting bizarre."

Not long after this incident, Justin Merriman was arrested on charges of battery and exhibiting a deadly weapon. It got him thrown into the California Youth Authority, and he was shipped off to Paso Robles, where he began his correspondence with Katrina Montgomery.

But Justin Merriman wasn't long for Paso Robles. His anger and rebelliousness would see to that. Early in the morning on July 3, 1990, one year to the day since the Davis incident, he was escorted with a group of other prisoners toward the showers. He claimed that he heard a couple of guards making derogatory remarks about his mother and sister. Merriman flew into a rage and suddenly struck Officer Paul Jones several times with his fists. CYA Officer Tim Brown came to Jones's assistance. The two officers attempted to wrestle Merriman to the ground, but he continued to kick and squirm beneath them. Officer Ed Burgh joined the melee and together they eventually restrained Merriman.

When Merriman was finally handcuffed, he was asked why he had assaulted an officer. Merriman replied, "Because [Jones] was talking about my sister and mother."

Jones denied making any derogatory comments.

For his outburst, Justin Merriman was found guilty of resisting and deterring an executive officer in the performance of his duties by force or threat of force. He was sentenced to two years in the California Department of Corrections, where he would serve his time at Corcoran State Prison when he turned eighteen years old.

While Justin Merriman was incarcerated in various institutions, he often wrote his mother letters. She was the one female he idealized. He treated girls his own age with contempt, but he had only politeness and true affection for his mother. In one letter, he wrote, "Mom, been talking to different people from different states other than good old California. Makes me think there is a better place than Ventura . . . but then again maybe it might be better for them, not for me. Guess it doesn't matter where you move if a person doesn't change his ways, right, Mom? We've talked about it many times."

He told her about a cellmate he had from Missouri who hated California. The cellmate complained that there seemed to be a cop behind every tree just ready to bust him. Justin laughed at this and said that the way this guy's mind worked, if you didn't see a cop you couldn't get into trouble. Then Justin admitted that it wasn't the cops that got him into trouble. It was himself.

"Oh well," he wrote, "it's enough on that and time to start

a letter to that little sister of mine. Have you been spending time together lately? That's important, Mom. Give her a call and do something together, OK?"

In another letter he wrote:

> Dearest Mom, it's your Tazmania [*sic*] Devil son coming at ya. That is the old monster in me you see [drawn] on the envelope. Doesn't that Taz look real pissed? I don't want to act that way around family and friends. This place makes me feel like roaring sometimes.

He told her when he had lunch he didn't eat any of it. Justin said the meat was rotten, but he would be out in sixty days. He added, "Like Tony the Tiger would say, 'That's grrreat!'"

In yet another letter he was effusive in his praise about the box of chocolates she had sent him. "Dear Mom, I don't know if it's all those rabbit turds I ate as a kid or all this candy and goodies I'm eatin' right now that's made me retarded. I'm stuck on stupid. This package you sent was straight up excellent. I wish I could have taken a picture of the smile on my face as I brought that big bag into the building. It was a Kodak memory like they say on the TV commercials."

He told her he had OD'd on the chocolate, but that was okay. None of the chocolate had melted, but he wouldn't have cared if it had. He said he would have scooped it up and eaten it anyway. "Oh man, Mom, I might really throw up, you know. I am going to lay my fat pot-bellied pig ass down right now. I just wanted to thank you for making me sick like this."

He also wrote her a letter complaining about the price of goods at the commissary. "What I've noticed this time here is the prices on the stuff in the commissary have went up big! Just candy bars went up to 60 or 65 cents each. They used to be 50 cents a pop. Oh my. Granola is a buck ninety a bag! What, is the King of the Jews running this place now?!!"

In all fairness, Beverlee Sue Merriman did write him some letters back telling him that he needed to straighten out his life. In one she wrote that she always wanted the best for him and Ember. She said she wasn't worried about Ember, but he was a different matter. She said that he didn't have the desire to go anywhere in life.

She told him that when he got home they would pick out the groceries for dinner and he could have the first supper for the rest of his new life. She said she was pleased that he would be totally free and on the way to a new start with new ideas and hopes for a better life together. She said, "I have been desperate to find the words to say and make you realize this new fresh start is really important. I would like to share a really good future. It is up to you how happy you will be."

Perhaps the most incredible letter from Justin to his mother is one he sent for Valentine's Day extolling the virtues of Adolf Hitler. He wrote:

> I'm reading an extremely good book. It's called *Hitler: The Path to Power*. I'll have to say the guy was quite a man. A hero in his own time before people started reading these lies them Jewish traitors wrote about him. That is the first thing I look for when picking out a book on the Nazis and National Socialist stuff, is the author. Very important to do so.
>
> Check the poem out the man himself wrote after his mother died.

Justin wrote her a translation of the poem that dealt with Hitler's realization that his mother was coming to the end of her life. It dwelt on her fading eyesight and memory and all the complaints of old age. Hitler recommended that a son should not be impatient with an elderly mother's infirmities, but rather help her and be understanding. If she demanded something, then the son should try and honor her request. The poem ended nearly in a sob when Hitler wrote:

> The hour will come, the bitter hour,
> When her mouth asks for nothing more.

"That kind of tripped on my mind a little," Justin said. "Gave me a touch of the blues so I thought I'd share it with you, so you could feel my woe, ya know."

Justin told her he'd also read some of Hitler's speeches, but she probably wouldn't be interested in them. Then he asked her if she was hip to a guy named Maurice Boring who wrote a book called *The Puppet Show of Memory.* He quoted a line from the book, which stated, "War is to man what motherhood is to a woman—a burden, a source of untold suffering, and yet a glory!"

"Kind of makes sense, doesn't it?" Justin wrote.

He asked her if she had ever read anything by Oswald Spengler when she was in school. Then he claimed he was getting an education in jail about history, science, and philosophy all from the books he was reading. Of course, they were all books that were sympathetic to the Nazi cause and the superiority of the white race.

Justin finished his letter by quoting Hitler once more:

> For us it is a problem that decides whether our people become internally healthy again, that decides whether the Jewish spirit will really disappear. Jewish influence will never disappear, and the poisoning of the people will not end, as long as the virus, the Jew, has not been removed from our midst!

Have a good Valentine's Day, 'cause your kid loves
you lots.
Justin.

By the time Justin Merriman hit the streets of Ventura
again after his release from Corcoran Prison, there was no
doubt how he felt about Nazis, skinheads, "inferior races,"
and how to treat young women his own age. Instead of stay-
ing away from the Skin Head Dogs, as the terms of his
probation demanded, he was right back with them stronger
than ever. It only took him until Halloween 1992 to get into
trouble with the law once again.

Merriman was at a rowdy party of skinheads in the city
of Fillmore when Deputy Sheriff Van Davis responded to a
call about all the noise. Davis heard trash cans being tipped
over as he arrived and then saw some men throwing punches
near the trash cans. Witness Joseph Urrea yelled to Davis,
"Hey, there they go! Get them!"

Davis saw Justin Merriman and Ethan Boyle jumping up
from a prone man who was lying on the ground. The man
turned out to be a Mr. Kutback, and by the time Davis got to
him, he was unconscious.

Deputy Davis drew his pistol and ordered Merriman and
Boyle to the back of the house. Merriman and Boyle were
both covered in blood and appeared to be quite intoxicated.
They were arrested for the incident and had something new
to add to their list of crimes.

As October turned to November in 1992, Justin Merriman
was a seething, angry young man. His time at Corcoran State
Prison had not diminished his aggressiveness. Anyone who
got in his way or spurned his sexual advances was in danger
of a beating or worse. Including Katrina Montgomery.

FIVE

ANATOMY OF A GANG

According to Ventura Police Department Lieutenant Ken Cornei, the skinhead gangs of Ventura were different than most street gangs. They were motivated more by hate and anger than the traditional protection of turf and drug sales. The gangs were very fluid, often adding new members as others moved away or dropped out of the scene. But one thing most of the members of the Ventura skinhead gangs had in common was a tendency toward sudden explosive violence. They could "go off" at any moment over the most trivial matter. In fact, they didn't need an excuse at all. Often they would attack a person who looked or acted differently from them. Especially if the person was Asian or African-American.

The Skin Head Dogs members were initially just a group of white fifteen- and sixteen-year-olds who hung out together, usually on Ventura Avenue just north of the old Buenaventura Mission. They did not develop in a vacuum. Gang trouble was swirling all around them in the late 1980s throughout Ventura County. Police said the problem was fueled by movies and music videos that glorified the gang lifestyle. These same agencies noted in 1990 that there were at least thirty-four gangs operating in the county. Within a short distance of downtown Ventura there were the Ventura

Avenue Gangsters, Haoles Hells Angels, Pierpont Rats, and East Side Saticoy Warlords. A little farther afield were the Oxnard Chicques, Trece Colonia Chicques, and Satanas.

Assistant Sheriff Oscar Fuller said, "[The gang members] have personalized their causes to where a grievance against an individual is a grievance against the whole group. It doesn't matter who you get revenge on, so long as you have revenge against the whole group."

Casiana Hollers could attest to that. She told a *Los Angeles Times* reporter that her boyfriend, Manuel "Deadeye" Rodriguez, had shouted his gang's name, the Lemonwood Chicques, in front of Channel Islands High School where some Satanas were loitering. A short time later, Satana member Arnel Salagubang confronted Rodriguez with a pistol. "Go ahead, shoot me if you dare," Rodriguez taunted him. Salagubang did, shooting Rodriguez in the head and killing him.

Hollers said, "[Rodriguez] told me a long time ago, 'If ever someone were to put a gun to my head, they'd better kill me, because if they don't I'll get back up and kill them.' I think he died for his pride. [The Satanas have] been coming by our house. Putting their fingers to their head and making like a gun and laughing. They're still going on with it, that their guys killed [him], and they're proud of it."

The article went on to portray gang members' mentality. It said that they had to be proud of their neighborhood, spray-paint walls and buildings to proclaim their turf, and fight back even when outnumbered. Most of all, they had to protect the homeboys and homegirls who lived in the 'hood. "Hit back anyone who disrespects you. Even kill."

Gang violence was starting to become a way of life in Ventura during those turbulent years. Roberta Payan, who got out of the life, was once a Ventura Avenue Gangster girl. She said, "There's kids out here who would just rather make a name for themselves by shanking [stabbing] somebody or killing somebody or making their mark. The little *pequenos* sitting around seeing the older gang members getting out of the joint with their tattoos and playing handball, they say, 'Wow, it's like cowboys and Indians.'"

A sixteen-year-old girl named Brenda, who was also a gang girl, concurred. She said, "We'd hit motorists with pipes and take their cars. Sometimes go on joyrides. Or get party money by stripping the cars and selling the used parts. I thought it was fun. Sometimes we'd do it for beer, a couple of rocks, cocaine . . . just have a party."

But these gang parties were always dangerous affairs and magnets for violence from other rival gangs. Edward Throop and other gang members were sitting around in a lemon orchard drinking with some girls when they decided to take a ride to Cabrillo Village. Throop thought it might be a good idea to test-fire a rifle they had just obtained. In a fit of drunkeness, he pulled out the semiautomatic rifle and fired randomly on a cul-de-sac in Cabrillo Village. His shots struck and killed eighteen-year-old Javier Ramirez, and twenty-year-old Rolando Martinez, who just happened to be in the wrong place at the wrong time and had no gang affiliations.

Even more egregious was a drive-by shooting at a birthday party on Houston Drive. Nineteen-year-old Scott Kastan came from a wealthy family in the area but decided to join a gang anyway. While out driving in an expensive BMW, he and other gang members spotted a rival gangster coming out of a residence on Houston Drive. While his friend drove, Kastan popped up through the sunroof of the BMW and took some shots at the rival gang member. But his aim was bad, and he struck and killed twenty-year-old Jennifer Jordan, the mother of a young child, instead.

* * *

All of this gang violence wasn't off in some distant area from Scott Porcho, Mitchell Sutton, and Justin Merriman. It was virtually in their backyard, up and down Ventura Avenue. Ventura police sergeant Earl Handy said of the environment along the Avenue, "It's being held hostage by these gangsters with guns. There's no gang war. It's just stupid acts of violence and random late-night shootings."

No one was safe from the gunfire along Ventura Avenue. Inebriated or drugged-up gang members fired at homes and parked cars for no reason at all. On one street in the neighborhood, police later found fifty spent shell casings littering the street. In such a deadly environment, it's little wonder that the original members of the Skin Head Dogs banded together for mutual protection. The only problem was that over time they became even more violent and dangerous than their rivals.

Michelle Conkle, a deputy probation officer who worked extensively with juveniles, remembered an incident in the late 1980s when the Skin Head Dogs first came on the scene. "[My office and police officers] first became aware of this bunch when we got a call about a wild party in Camarillo," a city a few miles from Ventura. "When officers arrived, it was pure pandemonium. There were over a hundred white teenagers there, many of them skinhead types, who were drinking, yelling, and fighting. The situation was totally out of control. They had practically destroyed the home of the kid whose parents owned the place. There were at least two stabbings by the time officers arrived, and numerous arrests as the kids turned upon the officers. It was a scene that anyone who was there would never forget. This was the first time I heard the names Scott Porcho, the Sutton brothers, and Justin Merriman. These were names I would know all too well in the next few years."

Just like Lieutenant Cornei, Deputy Probation Officer

Conkle saw that the Skin Head Dogs and their associates didn't have a cut-and-dried philosophy other than anger and hate. "If you were black or Asian and around them, then they just might attack you for no reason at all except for the color of your skin or ethnicity," she said. "They were incredibly violent. Into using their fists, chains, and especially boots. They liked 'booting' people. Kicking and stomping them with their Doc Marten boots. They might have picked this up from the British punk rock scene. They were definitely into that kind of violent music and anarchistic behavior. They were always having wild parties, and these parties were often broken up by police officers. I'd say that alcohol was their drug of choice. They would become incredibly drunk and think nothing of attacking each other and even police officers. It didn't take them much to become enraged. A lot of these kids were from broken homes, and there was a lot of anger just beneath the surface in these kids."

One person Conkle knew well was Scott Porcho. She considered him one of the most violent and dangerous members of the gang. "There was one incident that showed just how strong and maniacal this guy was. During a disturbance, Scotty attacked a police officer. The officer hit Scott over the head with his billy club. It didn't even faze him. It took several officers to restrain Porcho."

But two people Conkle remembered most from this period were Justin Merriman and his mother, Beverlee Sue Merriman. Especially Beverlee Sue. Conkle recalled, "I first became aware of Justin Merriman in 1988. He had been involved in numerous fights. At one particular party there was a stabbing, and I believe Justin was involved. He had received a cut on his leg during this party and had been brought into my office later. I asked him where he got the cut. Before he could even answer, his mother, who was there, began lying for him. She said he had fallen down and got the cut at home. I was sure this wasn't true. My biggest problem with Justin was his mother. With a lot of kids, if I could reach them early enough, I could turn them around. But it needs the cooperation of the parents. With Beverlee Sue Merriman, she could never admit that Justin did anything wrong. She made excuses for him all the time. In fact, she became almost a den mother for these Skin Head Dogs. Lending them money, taking them places. As far as I was concerned, she was just another Skin Head Dog member."

Beverlee Sue Merriman would later relate how she viewed Justin and his friends in the Skin Head Dogs. "These people were like a club," she said. "They gathered together and had some brews together. Like any Monday night football group. When people [like them] are cut off from what I consider this planet, I reached out and helped them."

This even included giving them money while they were in jail or prison. She said about this later, "I gave them money for commissary and for writing materials. For them to be able to write letters to their families. It wasn't a selfish thing on my behalf to do that. I wanted to do that so they could have things provided for them in prison. I encouraged all these kids, once they got out of prison, to do things correctly."

As far as her son's racist beliefs went, Beverlee Sue later said, "I encouraged him to read everything possible. I didn't believe any of [Hitler's] issues. But I was trying to get Justin to understand that I felt, too, that [Hitler] was out there trying to get money and hurt a lot of people. I don't approve of the things he did at that time. But I wanted Justin to read about it himself."

But Justin did more than just read about Hitler and the Nazis. He glorified them. And Beverlee Sue Merriman did very little to stop anything that Justin was adamant about.

* * *

In 1989, Ventura County officials started noticing a vast increase in skinhead activity. One of the first incidents that year was the trashing of an African-American teacher's home in Simi Valley while he was away on vacation. Drawers and cabinets were overturned; clothes, toys, and personal items were scattered everywhere and brown paint had been dumped in the clothes dryer and on the piano. The word "Nigger" was carved into the dining room table and graffiti was spray-painted on interior walls, including swastikas and the word "Skinheads."

Not far away, swastikas and anti-Semitic epitaphs were spray-painted on the back wall of a Jewish synagogue, Temple Ner Tamid. Soon thereafter, an eleven-year-old boy threw an egg at a woman entering the temple and called her a "kike."

Things were just heating up at this point in the county. Temple Beth Torah was vandalized in Ventura, with windows smashed and anti-Semitic graffiti painted on the walls. A classroom was riddled with air gun pellets.

Merriman's friends in the Skin Head Dogs were busy, as well. Nineteen-year-old Scott Porcho assaulted a boy on Ventura Beach with a rock and was arrested. Michael Vernon Fields, who was under the influence of cocaine, attempted to walk into a courtroom with a .357 magnum revolver. Skinheads robbed a liquor store, and when the Korean employee followed them out into the parking lot, they assaulted him with a baseball bat. The words "Skinz" and "White Power" were spray-painted all over a residential neighborhood in the Simi Valley.

When Jessie Roybal, a Native American living in Camarillo, complained to the police about the gang activity, she and her family were harassed by skinheads. She told the press, "Beer bottles are thrown at our house, obscenities are yelled at us; they've followed my daughter from the house to work. We've been called every name in the book."

Skinheads and neo-Nazis were so arrogant by the autumn of 1989 that they were handing out racist literature at the local high schools. Brochures and flyers were confiscated by officials, and some of the literature had ties to the White Aryan Resistance and National Socialist White American Party. Ventura County's district attorney, Michael Bradbury, said, "There is a growing pattern. We're seeing recruitment activities in high schools and also acquisition of deadlier weaponry. They're throughout the county."

The Simi Valley Police Department assigned a detective to work full-time on just hate crimes, as did the Ventura Police Department. By 1990, it was like trying to put their fingers in a crumbling dike. The skinhead problem was growing expotentially. A teenage girl was beaten with a baseball bat for attempting to leave a gang in Camarillo. Bomb threats were phoned in to the Verdugo Hills Hebrew Center. Temple Beth Torah in Ventura had "ZOG" (Zionist Official Government) spray-painted on its walls. Racist literature was stuffed into mailboxes and placed under vehicle windshield wipers. And Skin Head Dogs member Michael Wozney attacked a black member of the Ventura College basketball team with a bottle, and was arrested.

Eugene Mornell of the Los Angeles County Human Relations Committee told a *Los Angeles Times* reporter, "There are increased ethnic tensions on population shifts that have caused racial and ethnic minorities to move into what were once predominately white communities. Ventura County might be subject to the same increase in hate crimes affecting most cities in southern California. The recent spate of hate crimes, particularly in Simi Valley, does reflect something about the climate of those communities."

* * *

Investigator Mark Volpei had some interesting things to say about the Skin Head Dogs in particular. He wrote later in a court document, "The gang was formed by Scott Porcho and approximately six other people. The original formation of the gang was for protection of its members from Hispanic gangs on Ventura Avenue. Many original Skin Head Dog members resided on Ventura Avenue and they believed they were targeted by Hispanic gangs as individuals. The gang originally was a drinking, brawling gang that clearly followed the punk rock music culture. Eventually, some of the members began to introduce elements of white supremacy to the gang. The gang began to adopt symbols of Nazi Germany and other white supremacist organizations. As the gang grew in numbers, the violent acts the gang committed also grew.

"Skin Head Dogs members referred to themselves as brothers. Skin Head Dogs were exclusively a male organization and the members considered each other family. Women did associate with the gang, but the members of the Skin Head Dogs clearly put their members ahead of any woman. When an old member would bring a new member into the gang, the new member would be called the old member's 'kid.' If a member of the Skin Head Dogs became involved in a fight, it was incumbent on any other member to participate in the fight. It was a brotherhood which protected their own at all costs, and matched any violence with greater violence. If a gang member was facing criminal charges, other members would intimidate victims and witnesses to prevent testimony or provide false testimony to assist in the member's defense.

"The hierarchy of the gang was not well organized, but led by the oldest and most violent. Members of the Skin

Head Dogs would commit violent offenses, which led to a number of them suffering criminal convictions. These convictions would result in prison commitments for many of the members. If a Skin Head Dog member served a prison term, their status within the gang increased. Among Skin Head Dog members, it was a badge of honor and respect to complete a prison term. The prison culture soon became a part of the Skin Head Dogs, as more and more members began serving time in the Department of Corrections."

The prison gang in California that had first banded together for the advancement of white supremacy was the Aryan Brotherhood. It began in the 1960s, and by the 1970s it was busy recruiting new white members within the California Youth Authority. These were mostly sixteen- and seventeen-year-olds. But as authorities began to crack down on the Aryan Brotherhood, a new organization began to grow within the CYA. It was the Nazi Low Riders (NLR). Taking their name in part from the low-riding vehicles of southern California, they quietly organized while the authorities' attention was diverted toward the Aryan Brotherhood. The Nazi Low Riders were very secretive, tightly knit, and they managed to keep their affiliation secret for a number of years.

All of the early Skin Head Dog members eventually had contact with the Nazi Low Riders as they moved through the California Youth Authority. Originally, the Skin Head Dogs had been just a loose confederation of angry young white men interested in the violent side of the punk rock scene. But once they moved through the CYA, they began to adopt some of the Nazi Low Riders' racist and pro-Nazi rhetoric. Both groups had a hatred of people of color, calling them the "mud people." Their anger was particularly directed toward African-Americans and "race traitors"—people involved in interracial relationships.

The one ethnic group that the Nazi Low Riders, Aryan Brotherhood, and Skin Head Dogs did not discriminate against was Hispanics. Many of them had Hispanic girlfriends or wives, and a few members were even Hispanic themselves. In fact, most of the members of both groups came from poor white families that lived in predominately Hispanic neighborhoods. An alliance with Hispanic groups, such as the Ventura Avenue Gangsters, was a matter of survival.

Within prisons, the Nazi Low Riders was an extremely tight-knit organization and hard for law enforcement agents to infiltrate. Informants within the group were dealt with harshly. The members often passed kites (handwritten letters that went from cell to cell), using a secret code of runic symbols adopted from ancient German mythology. By the early 1990s, the authorities knew they had a new problem on their hands in addition to the Aryan Brotherhood. The Nazi Low Riders were causing serious disruptions and creating violence in the California prison system.

Just how tight the NLR is can be shown by its hierarchy. Each unit is led by a "senior" who has to have been a member for at least five years. He is "elected" to his post by three other seniors. Just below them in rank are the "juniors." These members of the Nazi Low Riders can try to recruit new members for the organization, but only seniors can bring them in. Once the new member joins, he is called a "kid," and it is the senior's responsibility to be his mentor and mete out discipline to him when the need arises.

In a mirror image of this practice, the Skin Head Dogs "seniors" recruited new members for their gang, and called their young protégé their "kids."

As the Skin Head Dogs' early members went through the

California Youth Authority in the late 1980s and early 1990s, they also began to adopt some of the Nazi Low Riders' symbols. There was no standard hat, jacket, or color that needed to be worn, but tattoos displaying swastikas, SS lightning bolts, iron crosses, and other Nazi symbols began to appear on Skin Head Dogs' faces and bodies. Eagles and skulls were also popular, as well as the member's gang nickname.

As the original wave of Nazi Low Riders members moved out of prison and back into the neighborhood, they kept their gang affiliation going as a street gang. And like the Skin Head Dogs, they weren't so much turf-oriented as they were hate-oriented. One of the first strongholds of the NLR was in Costa Mesa, California. Their violence against others fully came to light in 1996. Nazi Low Riders members Daniel Batoosing, Robert Harris, Kevin Camp, Matt Estrada, and John Savino attacked a twelve-year-old boy in a video arcade and nearly beat him to death with a pipe.

In Lancaster, California, Danny Williams and Eric Dillard, two racist gang members, beat a black teenager with a baseball bat because they saw him walking down the sidewalk. A few months later they stabbed a black man in the back. When arrested, Williams said he wanted to rid the streets of Lancaster of "niggers."

By the 1990s, the NLR was spreading throughout the West, especially in juvenile detention facilities. The FBI estimated that there were at least 1,500 members in California, a hundred in Nevada, and some even in Colorado and New Mexico. They had a dual purpose, to be the "home" for white prison inmates and to make money by drug trafficking. They became very proficient in the production and distribution of methamphetamine. In these operations, they had a loose affiliation with outlaw motorcycle gangs.

The Skin Head Dogs gang members were never deeply into the production or distribution of drugs. As Michelle

Conkle had said, their drug of choice was alcohol. While the Nazi Low Riders had a controlled violence in their operations, the Skin Head Dogs were more anarchic in theirs. In some ways they harkened back to the violent fringe of the British skins and punks of the 1970s. Drinking and fighting were their "recreational" activities.

But although they didn't generally use or distribute drugs, the Skin Head Dogs did have contact with Nazi Low Riders and considered them a "brother" organization with a common goal of white supremacy. In this regard, they followed the example of other southern California white gangs such as Public Enemy Number One and the Sylmar Family.

The Sylmar Family and the Nazi Low Riders had a very similar way of living once their members were out of prison and back on the streets. Both groups had many houses and apartment complexes that were filled with young white males sharing the same space. In essence, the gangs had become their families. They ate together, drank together, and fought together. It was almost tribal in its structure. Anger and violence fueled their reason to exist.

But white females were also a part of the scene for the Nazi Low Riders, Sylmar Family, and Skin Head Dogs. Within the Nazi Low Riders, there were girlfriends and wives who helped the males in drug operations, witness intimidation, and while the males were in prison. Some even took part in murders.

Skin Head Dog girls had similar roles. While not full-fledged members of the gang, they nonetheless held similar beliefs and prejudices. Some of these girls wore white supremacist and Nazi tattoos and were proud of their affiliation with the "Dogs." Some actively participated in criminal activities, and almost all kept contact with their male counterparts who were in prison or jail. One such girl was a friend of Justin Merriman's named Bridget Callahan. She had gone to St.

Bonaventure High School with Katrina Montgomery, and at an early age began hanging around with members of the Skin Head Dogs. And even more than Katrina, she adopted their racist ideas and gangster type of lifestyle. In the words of others, she "talked the talk and walked the walk."

In the years to come, some Skin Head Dog girls would be Justin Merriman's strongest allies, and Bridget Callahan was certainly one of them. A Skin Head Dog girl could expect protection from a Skin Head Dog male, but only up to a certain point. Within the hierarchy, males came first and females second. But just like the males, she was expected to distance herself from and intimidate all informants.

Mark Volpei wrote later in a court document, "As the prison culture influenced the Skin Head Dogs gang, the members would spread these beliefs throughout their community. Anybody who would cooperate with law enforcement was a rat, and the gang would physically beat anyone who was believed to have cooperated with law enforcement against one of their members. The gang would act on these beliefs, and those in the community on Ventura Avenue were aware that violent repercussions would follow any cooperation with law enforcement against the Skin Head Dogs."

Mark Volpei's interview of Scott Porcho was even more succinct on this point. "[Porcho] considered his fellow gang members family, brothers, and would do anything to protect his family. Mr. Porcho was close to Ms. Katrina Montgomery, even considered her to be a sister to him, but he believed that it was his duty to protect [Justin Merriman] over any woman. Mr. Porcho stated that Ms. Montgomery had been his friend since they both attended high school in Ventura. Ms. Montgomery had remained friends with Mr. Porcho after she moved from Ventura to Los Angeles with her family. [But] Mr. Porcho explained that Justin Merriman was his brother, and brothers came before sisters."

Just how pervasive skinhead crime had become by the early 1990s in Ventura County was highlighted by comments made by Sheriff Bob Brooks. He said, "We're getting more violent incidents from these groups than any other. And we're getting to know these individuals. I think the things that make them so distinct is the degree of hatred for everybody who is not just like them."

Ventura police lieutenant Gary McCaskill went even further in his comments. He said they would attack anybody, even people who did look and act like them. "I think when we deal with white supremacists, most of the crimes seem to generate out of some kind of anger. Where that wells up from or how race plays into it, I don't know. But it certainly seems to be a group of angry people."

Law enforcement noted the largest percentage of skinheads and white supremacist gang members was congregated along Ventura Avenue, stretching from Main Street in Ventura clear up into the Ojai Valley, thirty miles away. Right in the heart of Skin Head Dogs country. They surmised there were about one hundred and fifty full-time members, with hundreds of wanna-bes and hangers-on. When they congregated for their parties, there was hell to pay.

In her report on white power youth groups in Ventura County, *Los Angeles Times* reporter Anna Gorman wrote:

> It's a Thursday afternoon and a worried Ventura mother named Kari says she hasn't seen her teenage son for four days. He and his older brother drifted into the white power movement a few years ago, and she lost all control of them. Kari said that she didn't know what happened. She had never taught them to be racists, but she wasn't home as much as she should have been. When she began to hear about their racist beliefs she tried to stop them.

Kari talked to her sons about her own opinions, which were not racist, and tried to steer them away from their present course. She brought friends home who were of other races and ethnicities. She even took the boys to the Museum of Tolerance in Los Angeles. But nothing seemed to work. By the time the boys were in their midteens, it was already too late.

Near the Ventura Pier, Jeremy, along with other skinheads, assaulted a Latino couple and an African-American couple who were on their way home from homecoming dates. The skinheads threw a brick at them and were chanting epitaphs as they followed the couples toward their car. When the couples attempted to drive away, the skinheads kicked the car with their boots and beat it with a baseball bat.

Jeremy served six months for his part in the attack on the couples, but when he got out he stole a car and was sentenced to four years in the California Youth Authority. Meanwhile, Christopher was in and out of the house with his white power friends.

Gorman wrote, "Kari still hopes her sons will grow out of their racism. 'Their values are all screwed up,' she said. 'All I know is that I'm scared to death about my older son. And his brother is soon to follow if he doesn't get out of this.'"

Anna Gorman spoke face-to-face with a white power skinhead in one of Ventura's downtown parks. His name was Mike. She wrote that his head was shaved and he wore tattoos that depicted an iron cross with a swastika on his chest, along with the words "White Power." She said his stare was mean and he punctuated his sentences with clenched fists. He spoke admiringly of Adolf Hitler and predicted an eventual race war in America. In his ideal world, America would be rid of all blacks, Asians, and Mexicans.

"We were here first, and we are better," he told her.

SIX

A WEB OF DECEIT

After Katrina Montgomery's blue pickup was discovered in the underbrush at Angels Crest on the afternoon of November 28, 1992, it was towed by the Los Angeles Sheriff's Department to an impound lot. Later that day, a tow truck driver who worked at the lot noticed bloodstains in the back of the truck and told the authorities. Since Katrina Montgomery's family lived within the Los Angeles Police Department jurisdiction, the sheriff's department phoned and gave the LAPD the particulars about the situation. The case was handed over to the LAPD Missing Persons unit.

On November 29, officers from that unit drove up to Ventura to check out leads about Montgomery's disappearance. One of the first places they stopped was at the Merriman residence on Miller Court in Ventura. When Officer William Hiem knocked on the door, Beverlee Sue Merriman answered it. In the background, Officer Hiem could see and hear a young man cleaning the rugs. When he asked about this, Beverlee Sue Merriman told him that she had spilled coffee on the white rugs and they needed cleaning. Officer Hiem asked to come in, but Beverlee said she wouldn't let him without a search warrant. To Hiem's eyes, she appeared to be nervous and very evasive.

In response, Officer Hiem told her that Katrina Montgomery's family was very upset about her disappearance, and one of the last persons to see her had been Justin Merriman. He asked once again if he could come in. She responded, "Get a search warrant."

Officer Hiem stuck around the residence long enough to question the young man who had been cleaning the rugs when he exited the residence. But the young man refused to give his name or phone number. Frustrated by the lack of cooperation, Officer Hiem drove to Scott Porcho's house in Oxnard. There he questioned Scott Porcho, Apryl Porcho, and a housemate named John Cundiff about Katrina Montgomery. Hiem noticed there was a bloody towel in a bucket sitting in the house. When questioned about it, Scott Porcho said that there had been a card game on the night of the party, and Justin Merriman was accused of cheating. A fight broke out and Merriman received a cut to his forehead. That's where the blood came from, according to Porcho. He said that after the fight Apryl had driven Merriman home.

Officer Hiem asked if Apryl had driven anyone else to Merriman's residence. Scott Porcho lied and said that Justin Merriman was the only one she had taken there. When Officer Hiem questioned Apryl about this, she used the same lie.

At this point, Officer Hiem decided to question John Cundiff separately. Cundiff had a very different story to tell. He stated that the fight had actually been over Katrina Montgomery. He said that Larry Nicassio, Ryan Bush, and Justin Merriman had been hassling her all evening. Scott Porcho had intervened, and in the words of John Cundiff, "beat the hell out of all of them." It was during this fight, Cundiff said, that Merriman received his cut.

Cundiff's story about Apryl Porcho was also different. He said that she had driven Merriman, Nicassio, and Bush to Merriman's home that night. Then he added that Katrina

Montgomery had been very drunk at the party and left by herself. Just before leaving, she had received a phone call from Justin Merriman.

With all these discrepancies in the stories, LAPD requested that Scott Porcho and Apryl Porcho go to the Oxnard Police Department for further questioning. The Porchos agreed, and they were separated once they reached the station house. When confronted by John Cundiff's statements, Scott Porcho gave a new version of the fight with Justin Merriman, telling just enough of the truth about the party to make his story believable.

Officer: "What kind of clothes was Katrina wearing?"

Porcho: "Black top that was low cut. Later on that night, when she was getting ready to go to bed, she borrowed one of Apryl's extra toothbrushes and she had taken a shower and she was wearing shorts or boxers. I wasn't sure what they were. And then when her and Apryl started arguing, she changed again to leave."

Officer: "Okay. So that was three times."

Porcho: "Twice. She came originally in something, changed into the shorts, then changed into something to leave."

Officer: "And when she was leaving, what was she wearing?"

Porcho: "I'm not really sure. I didn't get a look. I looked over to see her leaving and she was behind the lattice, and it looked like she was wearing dark clothes."

Officer: "And the argument was . . . Can you give us a brief synopsis of what happened?"

Porcho: "Uh, Trina yelled at Apryl, saying Apryl was trying to control her life. I think it had something to do with the fact that Apryl took Justin home and Trina wanted to talk to Justin, and Apryl wouldn't let Trina talk to him.

She wanted him out of there. And didn't want them to-gether. Then Apryl started yelling at Trina, saying, 'You compare me to your friend Shawna, and I'm not Shawna. You can't talk to me like you talk to Shawna.'"

Officer: "Okay, Shawna's another friend of your wife's?"

Porcho: "No, another friend of Trina's, who Trina doesn't, I don't think, talk to anymore, the last I heard. Shawna owed her money and wasn't friends with her anymore."

Officer: "You mentioned something about Justin and Trina trying to get together and talk . . . about the past or something."

Porcho: "I don't know what they were trying to talk about. Trina kept saying I gotta talk to him. Justin kept saying keep her away from me. Before the party started that night, before Trina even got there, I told Justin that Trina was gonna be there. And he's all, 'Ahh, no, just keep her away from me. Promise you'll do that?' And I go, 'Yeah, I'll keep her away from you.'"

Officer: "Let's back up just a little bit. Can you tell me a little bit about their relationship prior to their coming to the party?"

Porcho: "She used to go out with a friend of mine, Mitch Sutton, who I haven't talked to in a couple of years now. But Mitch hung out with me and Justin when we were younger. Well, when Mitch went in the army, Trina hung out with Justin and Ryan. And a couple of my friends. And they got to be close friends. Well, Mitch and Trina broke up. Justin went to the pen and Trina wrote him every day. Went and seen him. Took care of him real good. You know, a real close friend. Well, Justin thought, when I get out this is my girl-friend. She didn't want nothing to do with him when he got out. And he was kinda upset about that. And he's like, well, what do you want from me?"

Officer: "How long did that happen?"

Porcho: "Oh, he's been home about nine, ten months."

Officer: "So, then, they had been in communication till about nine or ten months ago?"

Porcho: "Yeah."

Officer: "Do you know if they've been in contact with each other since he got out of the joint?"

Porcho: "Yeah. I know he's talked to her on the phone."

Officer: "There's been no visits or anything like that?"

Porcho: "I don't think he's ever been to her house. I'm almost sure she's been at his house."

Officer: "Okay, go ahead. What was [Montgomery] wearing?"

Porcho: "I wasn't sure what she was wearing. But I looked up and she already had the door open and was looking back at Apryl, and Apryl was standing almost in the kitchen. And [Montgomery's] exact words were, 'Fuck, Ventura. I'm through with this town.' And she slammed the door behind her. And I'm positive I heard her truck start."

Officer: "Did the truck sound like it was leaving at a high rate of speed?"

Porcho: "I don't know if she was mad. As a matter of fact, I know she didn't drive off real fast."

Officer: "Okay, tell me about Trina's mom calling you and asking about her daughter. What's the first time that you know of when Trina's mom called?"

Porcho: "I called . . . no, my wife called the next day after the party, on Saturday . . . oh, I'm not even sure. It was anywhere between one and four o'clock in the afternoon."

Officer: "Saturday. That would have been [November 28], right?"

Porcho: "Right. And she said, I don't know where Trina is, I haven't seen her since Friday morning. Apryl said she's not here. We haven't seen her. Because when she left, the last thing we knew that she had said [was] she was going . . . her plan of action was to go see a guy that she knew in Santa Barbara. And she was supposed to go to her grandmother's house."

Officer: "And what is his name?"

Porcho: "I can't remember his name. I didn't know his last name. If you told me his name, I'd say, yeah, that was it."

Officer: "Was it Keith?"

Porcho: "That's it."

Officer: "Does he live in Ventura or Oxnard?"

Porcho: "Supposedly in Santa Barbara. She's a friend of his. I've never met him. I don't know what he looks like. She was supposed to meet him at his grandmother's house for something. I think my wife may have talked to him. Because he was doing a portfolio of modeling. And he wanted to take pictures of my wife. And Trina had asked my wife if she wanted to do it. And my wife, she's been in magazines before. Like, years ago when she was eighteen. And she'd done modeling and everything. But it never went through. He just decided he didn't want to do it. Trina's a photographer, too."

Officer: "Yeah, I heard that. Did she have any camera equipment with her when she left?"

Porcho: "Not that I know of. I didn't see any that night. She's a waitress, and photography's like a hobby."

Officer: "Where does Justin live?"

Porcho: "He lives in the east end of Ventura, by the government center. It's like a housing tract with real nice town houses."

Officer: "All right, when [Katrina's] mother called, what was the reason for not telling her that she was at the party?"

Porcho: "Because she was supposed to be going to see this guy in Santa Barbara. And we didn't know if she was supposed to be there, or here, or what she had told her mother she was doing. And we didn't wanna give her mother a different story than what she gave her mother."

Officer: "What was her relationship to you?"

Porcho: "You know, someone to talk to, 'cause you're being yelled at by your mom for something you did wrong. We called each other."

Officer: "So you confided in each other."

Porcho: "Yeah. We were just good friends."

Officer: "And your wife, was she jealous of her?"

Porcho: "After we got married. Before we got married, that was fine. There was no problem with that. When my wife and I were just boyfriend and girlfriend, she knew that Trina stayed at my house, and she knew there was nothing going on."

Officer: "Well, at the party was Trina friendly to you?"

Porcho: "Yes. As a matter of fact this is the first time that I've been around Trina that my wife didn't get mad about it. But then again, I haven't seen Trina in a long time. She lives in L.A. She used to live in Ventura. And that's where I first met her. She still comes to Ventura. But not as much as when she used to come and see her boyfriend."

Officer: "Who was her boyfriend?"

Porcho: "Mitch Sutton. The last time I saw him was about a month ago and I think he gave her a black eye. He beat her up and she broke up with him."

Officer: "Where does this Mitch Sutton live?"

Porcho: "I have no idea. I don't like him. I really don't like him. None of my friends like him. She would not let me know where he lived, or have his phone number."

Officer: "How do you know he beat her up?"

Porcho: "She told me. The last time I saw her, a month ago. And he beat her up about two weeks before I saw her. He lived either on the east end of Ventura or lived in Oxnard. But . . . I don't think he had anything to do with this."

Officer: "Now, why did he beat her up?"

Porcho: "She was at a party down at the beach and I guess she walked in a room and he was lying passed out on the bed. And he got up and looked at her and said get me a beer. And she was drunk, and she started mouthing off to him and telling him he was nothing, that he was gonna be a drunk like his father, and he socked her. She grabbed her stuff, got in the car, and left. She said that was it. I don't know, I guess that was the last time she saw him."

Officer: "Okay. Can you think where Trina might be?"

Porcho: "If her car wasn't wrecked, I could probably name a couple of places. But now that her car's been found, I have no idea . . ."

Officer: "What are you thinking?"

Porcho: "I keep hoping, but I think she's dead."

Officer: "Why do you think that? Be honest."

Porch: "Honestly, I don't want to know. I don't think it's anybody I know. Heck. It could look like I did it. It could look like Apryl did it."

Officer: "Uh-huh."

Porcho: "That's what I was telling Apryl. I go, we're suspects. We're the last people that saw her."

Officer: "Like we mentioned before, if you're holding back information you're gonna be implicated in a homicide if she is dead."

Porcho: "Yeah. Accessory to murder. I'm aware of that."

Meanwhile in another room, Apryl Porcho continued with her lies about the evening in question, not knowing that Scott Porcho had decided to tell more of the truth. She particularly persisted in her story about the card game causing the fight between Scott and Justin, not knowing that her husband was now telling a different version. She also continued to make up stories about the phone calls between their household and Katrina's mother.

Officer: "Okay, so you're visiting, and Trina's going back and forth. Is she drinking?"

Apryl: "I saw her drink. I don't know how many."

Officer: "Beer?"

Apryl: "Yeah. We usually don't have mixed drinks."

Officer: "She wasn't what you'd call drinking a lot?"

Apryl: "Yeah. She was still walking, talking, doing all that good stuff. She wasn't like slurring or being ridiculous."

Officer: "What was she doing about two o'clock?"

Apryl: "Everybody's sitting around playing cards."

Officer: "Was she playing cards?"

Apryl: "I think she was. She was in that room, and then she was in the living room. She usually doesn't sit still. We talked off and on. I was getting really tired, 'cause I had this cold. Then it was after four and I took Justin home like at 4:45 A.M., something like that."

Officer: "Why did you take Justin home, and Scott didn't?"

Apryl: "Scott doesn't have a driver's license . . . so it was like about five when I got home."

Officer: "Katrina's still there?"

Apryl: "She's still there."

Officer: "What is she doing?"

Apryl: "She was in the card room, and then, I walked into my room . . . Before I left she was saying she wanted to go. I told her I wanted her to stay. Then she got in her pajamas. I came back and she was dressed. Go figure. She's stubborn. She just does what she wants. She's very independent. She was [now] wearing tennis shoes, and overalls, and a T-shirt. And she says, why are you trying to run my life? I wanna leave. I'm like, I haven't seen you. I want you to stay. You know, after you've been friends for a while you get bitchy with each other because you have a million different things you can bring up and get mad at each other about, that you've dug up before. She used to have a friend named Shawna, I guess who used to screw her over and use her. And I just started yelling, look, I'm not Shawna. I don't want your damn money. I don't want you for rides. I don't want the damn pool in your house. I got a better car. I got just as much or more money than you. I've got my own damn pool. I was yelling, and go, okay, fine, just leave then. And she left."

Officer: "Okay, when's the next time you heard anything about Katrina?"

Apryl: "It's when I called her mom to see if she had went home. To see if she was still mad at me."

Officer: "Tell me about that conversation."

Apryl: "It was in the morning. It wasn't noon yet. I figured Trina went home. I figured she got pouty and went home. And I wanted to talk to her and see if she was still mad. I called and said, is Trina there? And she says, no, and I go, well, do you know where she is? And her mom says she's up in Santa Barbara for some family thing. She'll be back some time Sunday. And I'm like, okay. And then I didn't hear from [Katrina]. I didn't hear from her and I figured if she went to Keith's house she'd call me. And I felt dumb calling again after her mom just said, well, she's not here. So I asked Scott to. [I said] Scott, call Trina for me. And he called her and that's when her mom said they found the truck and it was over the side of a hill. I just flipped. I was like, my God, they found her truck abandoned. She's nowhere to be found. I just freaked out 'cause you hear the story all the time. Oh, we found this car abandoned, and then however many days later they find the driver, and usually they're not alive."

Officer: "At what point did her mother talk to you personally and ask you if she had been to the party?"

Apryl: "She called me after she talked to Scott. I didn't know what to say. It's not like Trina's mom and I have ever been old buddies. It's not like we've always hit it off or anything. So I just panicked. She's like, have you seen Trina? I could tell she was upset. I'm like, no, I haven't seen her. I should have said, yeah. But I just didn't know what to say. I was in shock. It's not like friends of mine disappear all the time. I just got really worried."

Officer: "You know, the logical question is, when somebody calls and says, hey, she's missing, we found her truck, was she at your house? The obvious answer would be, yeah. She was. She left here at five o'clock. I don't understand why you lied."

Apryl: "Well, I had a weird feeling. Her mom never calls me and talks to me. I just panicked. And I just started asking her all these questions. Was the truck wrecked? What happened? She said the keys were in it, and it was wedged at a forty-five-degree angle. I just got really upset. And I didn't wanna talk to her anymore. I just wanted to get off the phone. I didn't wanna deal with it. Just kinda block it out. I'll just hang up. Trina will call me later. She's fine, you know what I mean?"

Officer: "Yeah, right. Do you in some way feel responsible for this?"

Apryl: "Why should I?"

Officer: "Well, 'cause maybe you had the fight. She left and . . ."

Apryl: "I can't say that I don't feel bad in some way. Because maybe if we hadn't fought, maybe if she hadn't left, then maybe she wouldn't be missing. I wish she would have just stayed the night."

Officer: "Do you know of anybody wanting to hurt her?"

Apryl: "No. I don't, I can't see anybody wanting to hurt her. She's not that kind of person that people wanna . . . I mean, she's stubborn. She sometimes has a little temper and all. But I can't imagine . . . 'cause she's really pretty. And everybody likes her. As far as I know. If anybody has a secret thought to want to hurt her, it's unbeknownst to me."

After this interview, Scott Porcho's parole was deemed to be violated for lying to the police, and he was sent back to jail. They also contacted Justin Merriman's parole officer to check about him.

On November 30, the same day Nicassio and Bush were burying Katrina Montgomery's body at Sunset Farms, officers of the LAPD robbery/homicide unit showed up at Justin Merriman's door and conducted a parole violation search. One of the detectives was African-American, and Justin was less than pleased at his presence.

The detectives discovered freshly cleaned rugs and carpets. Detective James Harper said, "[Merriman's] room was immaculate, freshly cleaned, nothing out of place." This was in stark contrast to the rest of the house, which was fairly messy. A knife was discovered in Justin's room and he was deemed to be in violation of his parole.

On December 1, 1992, Justin Merriman was interrogated by Detective James Harper of the LAPD at the Ventura County Main Jail. They sat in a room typically used by defense attorneys to talk with their clients. Detective Harper already knew about Merriman's phone conversation with Katy Montgomery, Katrina's mother, and he attempted to find out what else Merriman knew about Katrina's disappearance. At this point, Justin was being treated as a witness rather than a suspect.

During the interview Justin said he had known Katrina Montgomery for four or five years, and that he'd last seen her at Scott Porcho's party on November 27. He thought she'd driven to the party in a blue pickup truck and that there had been between ten and fifteen people at the party. He said he knew all the Skin Head Dogs members there, but there were other people there he didn't know. He said he'd talked to Trina for a short while at the party, but that he didn't socialize with her because "she was a bitch." He said he tried to avoid her at the party as much as possible, and did not mention anything about the steak knives or what he had told Nicassio and Bush.

Then Justin used the agreed upon lie that he'd gotten into a fight with Scott Porcho over a card game. He said he'd been cut, and he lied that Apryl Porcho drove him home alone. In fact, he said, he hadn't had any visitors all of November 28.

Merriman asked to leave the interview, and since there was no probable cause to hold him, he was allowed to go.

On December 9, 1992, LAPD officers spoke with Ryan Bush in Sylmar. He told them about going to Porcho's party in Oxnard, along with Larry Nicassio and some other Sylmar Family skinheads. He related that he'd had a lot to drink at the party and decided to stay in Ventura instead of returning to Sylmar. He told of being given a ride to Justin Merriman's house, along with Larry Nicassio, by Apryl Porcho, thus contradicting Justin's story. He said they'd spent the night there and then paged Wayne Gibson the next day to come and pick them up.

Ryan Bush was given a lie detector test by the LAPD, and he flunked.

On that same day Wayne Gibson was interviewed by LAPD officers and admitted to being at Scott Porcho's party on the twenty-seventh. But he said he'd left early because of the fight between Porcho and Ryan Bush. He told the officers he had gone home to sleep, and lied that he returned to Ventura after being paged by Bush to give him and Larry Nicassio a ride back from the Merriman residence on the morning of the twenty-eighth.

While Gibson was being questioned, Ryan Bush called Larry Nicassio's cousin, Michelle Farnsworth. He told Farnsworth, "If the police question you, stick to story number one."

By now the blood in the back of Katrina Montgomery's pickup had been analyzed and tested for a possible DNA match to Montgomery. But Katrina Montgomery had no known blood samples on file, so the DNA patterns had to be matched to those of her parents. When this was done, it was determined that the blood in the pickup came from a child of Katy Montgomery and in all probability belonged to Katrina Montgomery.

After trying to lift fingerprints and blood samples from the pickup, which they had trouble doing because of the paint thinner, the LAPD released the truck to Mike and Katy Montgomery. But because it now had such bad memories for them, they decided to sell it. After they did, the only forensic evidence from the pickup left to the LAPD was a match to the Montgomerys' DNA and some pink fibers stuck in the pickup bed. These seemed to be fibers that might have come from a blanket.

On February 22, 1993, LAPD officers interviewed Michelle Farnsworth, Larry Nicassio's cousin. She told them that she had received a phone call from Nicassio early in February, asking her to give him a ride home from his grandmother's house. Since she was already in bed, she didn't want to go get him. But Nicassio kept begging her and finally she gave in.

Once she'd picked him up, he had her take winding roads, side streets, and even backtrack over the route they'd driven. She was already aware that he and Ryan Bush were suspects in the disappearance of Katrina Montgomery. Everyone among her friends had been talking about it. Farnsworth began to suspect that all the evasive driving had something to do with the missing girl and that perhaps he was taking her to see a body. When she asked where Nicassio was taking her, he answered, "You don't want to know."

Finally they approached an isolated area known as Sunset Farms. Nicassio had her drive slowly through the area, and when she asked what he was looking for, he answered, "Police tape."

On March 3, 1993, Detective Harper was finally able to question the young man Officer Hiem had seen cleaning carpets on November 30, 1992, at the Merriman residence. His name was Judson Mashburn and he said he occasionally cleaned carpets for Mrs. Merriman. Mashburn said he'd been called that morning in November by Mrs. Merriman to come over and clean the carpets. He told Detective Harper he didn't see anything unusual that day, only coffee stains on the carpet.

On March 24, 1993, Larry Nicassio was questioned for the first time by the LAPD. He stuck with the story that he and Ryan Bush had concocted about spending the night at Merriman's place and then paging Wayne Gibson to pick them up the next day. He also said he had no idea about the whereabouts of Katrina Montgomery. But he did add a new twist to the story. He said after being picked up by Gibson on November 28, he'd gone to Disneyland.

On April 20, 1993, the LAPD reinterviewed Wayne Gibson, prior to his being sentenced in an unrelated felony case. This time Gibson admitted that he'd made up the story about being paged to go to Ventura to pick up Nicassio and Bush.

He said they had actually come to his house. But he said he'd done this on his own and no one had put him up to it. Then Gibson told the truth about Ryan Bush asking to borrow his pickup on the twenty-eighth. He recalled that Bush returned with it at least seven hours later. Where Bush had gone with the pickup, Gibson said he had no idea.

Even though the LAPD searched the Sunset Farms area, they did not discover a fresh grave or Katrina Montgomery's body. There seemed to be a lot of lying going on between members of the Skin Head Dogs about Katrina Montgomery's last known movements. But in the official records, she was still just a missing person. It was a case that was going nowhere fast.

In an effort to jump-start something, Councilwoman Ruth Galanter pushed through a $10,000 reward from the Los Angeles City Council for information leading to the location of Katrina Montgomery. The reward statement read, "She is a twenty-year-old Westchester woman. She was last seen leaving a party in Oxnard to drive home alone. Her pickup truck, a blue Toyota, was found abandoned the next day in Angeles National Forest, near Little Tujunga Canyon Road. A student at Santa Monica College, Montgomery is 5 feet, 3 inches tall and weighs about 120 pounds. She has red hair and brown eyes. Anyone with information on the case may call LAPD Detective Bill Hiem or Detective Fred Miller."

But even the offer of a reward didn't do much good. Every day of waiting at the Montgomery home was like a weight of lead placed upon them. There were many days that Katrina's mother could not even get out of bed. At least Katrina's father, Michael, had the distractions of work to keep him busy. He said later, "It was a period of confusion. In my mind, though, I wasn't very confused. I'm a civil litigator and I deal with traumatic injury cases. I see tragedy day in and day out, and because of what I do for a living, I have become very proficient at compartmentalizing. Early on I realized that things didn't look very good. At that point, rather than pursue the many channels of hope that many of my family members followed, I turned my focus on my remaining two children and made a conscious effort to make sure that their lives remained as normal as one could make them under the circumstances. In some respects, it helped me deal with the loss of my daughter. In other respects, it hindered it. By compartmentalizing, I was able to distract myself and focus on other areas—my career, my other children. It doesn't mean there wasn't a dark cloud every day hanging over my life and the life of my family."

Michael Montgomery may have tried to create a normal life for his remaining two children, but there was no more normality left in the Montgomery household for anyone. Katrina's sister, Laurie, was thirteen years old at the time. She had adored her big sister and spoke of the way Katrina had helped her paint her fingernails and had picked her up from dance class. For some psychological reason, Laurie started stashing junk food in her bedroom, thinking that Katrina would come home and be hungry for it.

But day after day Katrina did not come home, and Laurie later said, "I think as time went on, all of us knew she wasn't coming home."

Brother Vaughn, who was one year older than Laurie, agreed. "We lost hope of ever finding her alive. We had to swallow, in whatever foggy, unclear way we could, that she was gone."

As time went on their hopes shifted to other areas—finding her body and finding her killer. But even in this, one year passed to the next with no new clue as to where her body might be located.

In the interim since 1992, Justin Merriman had been busy, as well. He'd been busy beating up people, spreading hatred, sexually abusing young women, and being tossed back in jail.

SEVEN

"I'LL SLICE YOUR THROAT LIKE I DID TO TRINA."

Katrina Montgomery was not the first or last woman that Justin Merriman sexually abused. As early as the mid-1980s he had been abusive toward women he knew in the area. A Ventura girl named Dorothy Slater met Justin in 1984 when he was twelve years old, and said she had "an on-again, off-again" relationship with him through 1991. She described her sexual relationship with Justin as "consensual but scary." He became menacingly violent with her during intercourse, "slapping me, pulling my hair, and fighting."

Even in public he was crude to her. He would pull her pants down in front of his friends, and even locked her in a pantry closet for hours. Merriman repeatedly poked her in the chest with his finger and would pin her to the floor with his body. When she told him to stop, he just laughed at her.

Merriman always wanted to have anal sex with her, much to Slater's distaste. During her last sexual encounter with him in 1991, he wanted another man to join them in the sexual experience. When she refused, they both masturbated in front of her.

A few years earlier, possibly in 1988, Justin Merriman

was also dating Theresa Baldini. She was fifteen years old at the time and he was sixteen. Already a member of the Skin Head Dogs, Justin Merriman was continually abusive toward her. He once knocked her down in a city park, and when she tried to rise he knocked her down again. He kept at it until Scott Porcho intervened and made him stop. Up to a point, Scott Porcho would protect women and girls from Justin's depredations.

Theresa Baldini recalled one incident in Ojai when she and Justin were both in a sports utility vehicle. He would not let her out of the vehicle and she began to get scared. He became "very forceful with his hands," she remembered, "and would not let me leave." He kept demanding sex, and she said later, "If I didn't let him, it was gonna get bad." She gave in and they had intercourse.

There was a short hiatus in Merriman's abuse when his parole had been violated for having a knife in his possession, found when the LAPD investigators were looking into Katrina Montgomery's disappearance at the end of 1992. But even when he went back to prison, he didn't sweat it too much. As he wrote to his mother in a couple of letters about this incarceration, "After getting out of fish row on C-Yard, I'm moving to the best yard at this place, B-Yard. Oh, I'm set to be rolling Cadillac style from here on out! Told you I would be. I want you to know you're missed and loved. Not too much longer until I'm home. I'm gonna have to go to the movies with you. Have you got my gun from my friend yet? He should be done with fixin' it by now I'm sure."

He asked her about Ember and how Christmas had been. Then he complained that he had to borrow Walkmans from others around the jail because his own wasn't working. He said he listened to some old punk tapes that he borrowed and wanted her to go to Radio Shack to pick up a new Walkman and some KD sunglasses for him.

Then he wrote that he was only going to "kick back" with the white boys who had helped him out when he didn't have anything. He said that in a couple of weeks he would really be rolling and that he couldn't believe his incarceration was because of a parole violation. But he added that it would be easy for him and sympathized with a cellmate who was looking at seventeen years. By comparison he said, "I think of that and all this stuff seems like puppy piss. I'm feeling pretty good and will be home with Mama real soon."

In fact, he was home with more than Mama "real soon." After he got out, Justin did not change one iota in the way he treated young women around Ventura. His abuse of women became even more pronounced. A young woman named Sally Crocker had known Merriman since she was eighteen years old in 1988. She had been married to a Skin Head Dogs member, got divorced, and dated around. Eventually she had a baby by another Skin Head Dogs member named Larry Mason in 1991. Larry was a good friend of Justin Merriman, and in 1992 he was sent to prison on a charge unrelated to the Katrina Montgomery case. It gave Merriman a good opportunity to make his move on Crocker.

While Mason was in prison, Crocker began to have consensual sex with Justin Merriman. In the initial phase, she enjoyed his company because he was protective of her and spent money on her. Then in 1993, Merriman slapped her for the first time because he was drunk and the baby's crying annoyed him. They exchanged words and he hit her in the face, saying, "You don't know when to shut up sometimes."

Another Skin Head Dogs member was there at the time and told Merriman to leave. As he did, Justin said to Crocker, "You'd better not call the police."

Sally Crocker noticed that Merriman's behavior changed for the worse after Katrina Montgomery's disappearance. He became more paranoid and seemed to fly off the handle for no reason. He began showing up at her apartment all hours of the day and night, demanding sex. He wouldn't take no for an answer and slapped her around until she submitted.

Of one attack Crocker said, "I gave in to him. He didn't beat me up or nothing. I just wasn't going to get him mad. Hit me or worse. Knowing what he did to Trina."

By now, it was common knowledge among gang members and their girlfriends about what Merriman had done to Katrina Montgomery. He also made it very plain what would happen to them if they ever told the authorities.

During one sexual assault on Crocker he kicked open a side gate at the apartment and began pounding on her door. Crocker decided to let him in before he broke down the door. While her daughter slept, Merriman kept following Crocker around the apartment, becoming more insulting with each step. She told him to leave but he refused. He backed her into the bedroom where her daughter was sleeping and Crocker began to cry and pleaded with him to stop.

She recalled, "I just gave up. I was scared. I couldn't get rid of him. I knew what he wanted. So I just gave in."

When he was finally through having sex with her, she cried, "Please leave."

Merriman snarled back, "Quit being a sorry bitch. I'll choke you out if you ever tell Mason or anyone else what I did."

This kind of harassment went on for months. Crocker never knew when Merriman might show up to sexually attack her. He would often pop the sliding glass door on the side of the apartment and let himself in, day or night. She was scared to tell the police about it for fear of retribution.

On one occasion she was taking a shower when Merriman broke in and told her he wanted sex. Crocker told him she didn't want to and wrapped a towel around herself. But

Merriman blocked her way and ripped off her towel. He raised his hand to slap her and she flinched. He began to laugh. "Why are you so afraid of me?" he asked. Then without another word, he left.

Merriman's abuse of Crocker only increased as time went by. He would pop either the windows or the sliding glass door and let himself in. By 1995 Crocker noticed that his drug use was becoming more pronounced, which only fueled his violence. As she said, "During this time he got really, really weird."

Merriman would force her into the bedroom and have sex with her for hours. While making her perform, he would look at pornographic magazines or videos. She pleaded with him that she was too sore to continue. But he either laughed at her or told her to shut up and keep going.

To control her, Merriman said that none of his friends would believe her if she ever told about the assaults. "They'll call you a liar and a whore. If you ever tell the police I'll wring your neck."

Even when she wasn't home, Justin Merriman inflicted his depradations on Sally Crocker. He would break into her apartment when she was gone and steal things to sell for his drug habit. Later he told her he didn't know why he did it, other than that he was high at the time and needed the money.

After a few years went by, Larry Mason was released from prison and came home. But even then Mason didn't protect Sally Crocker. He was out getting drugs too often, and Justin Merriman knew just when Mason was high and away from the apartment. On those occasions, Justin still came by to assault Crocker. During one of these episodes, Crocker said, she was in the bedroom when Merriman arrived, demanding sex. Things had degenerated so far that she recalled, "It wasn't so bad this time, because there were other people in the house." In other words, he didn't slap her around while having sex.

On another occasion in either October or November of 1995, she recalled a Sunday morning when Merriman broke in. Her daughter was at her mother's house and she was taking a nap on the couch. Merriman sat down beside her on the couch and placed a blanket over both of them. Then he unzipped his pants and placed her hands on his penis. When she resisted, he pulled her hair and twisted her head toward his penis. As she struggled, he yelled at her and twisted even harder. Finally out of fear that he might kill her, Crocker gave in and orally copulated him.

After this, Crocker went into her daughter's room, but the assault didn't stop there. Merriman ripped off her clothes, even though she told him that her mother and daughter would be back soon. But he didn't care and proceeded to rape her.

One of the most painful attacks Crocker recalled was an occasion when she had stopped by Merriman's home. He forced her into his bedroom and literally tackled her when she tried to leave, pining her to the floor and raping her there.

The last incident occurred in 1997. Crocker couldn't remember the exact date but it was around 3:00 A.M. Crocker didn't want him in the house, so she stepped outside with him. Merriman cajoled her into his car and drove off at a high rate of speed. When she asked where they were going, he replied, "I've got a hole for you in the desert."

Crocker became extremely frightened and told him to stop the car. But Merriman refused. In desperation, she said she would jump out of the speeding vehicle if he didn't stop. Surprisingly, Merriman slowed down and took her home.

Even while he was abusing Sally Crocker, Justin Merriman was also assaulting a girl named Sandra Elmwood. In the winter of 1994, Elmwood was twenty years old and living on her father's boat in Ventura Harbor. The boat was used as a party boat by young people and drugs were taken there. Elmwood in particular was often strung out on heroin and methamphetamine. She knew Justin Merriman from occasions where they'd been at the same house in Ventura using drugs.

Elmwood recalled an incident in 1994 when she and Merriman were in one of the state rooms on her father's boat doing drugs. There were other young people on the boat, but Elmwood and Merriman ignored them. They were busy fondling each other on the bed. Then she remembered, "Things got weird."

Merriman barricaded the door and would not let Elmwood leave. He demanded that she do everything that he wanted or else. This list of desires included oral sex, vaginal sex, and anal sex. He looked at pornographic magazines while he forced her to masturbate him. He called her a slut and a whore all the while. He made her orally copulate him until her mouth was sore. Her overall assessment of Justin Merriman that day was, "He was violent and crazy."

When Justin Merriman wasn't abusing Sally Crocker or Sandra Elmwood, he was taking out his sexual abuse on Andrea Morrow. Morrow had met Merriman in a drug house in Ventura, and they were both using meth. One night after a party, she went to Merriman's house at about 11:00. She was ready to have consensual sex with him, but instead he injected some kind of narcotic into her arm, possibly heroin, and things, in her words, "began to get very weird."

He ordered her around, told her to get undressed and lie on his bed. Then he pulled out some pornographic magazines, lay down next to her, unzipped his pants, and forced her to masturbate him. He held on to her hand with one of his while holding the magazine in another. Morrow said this went on literally for hours.

Merriman could not maintain an erection the whole time, but Morrow was so scared she kept trying to masturbate him. She knew the rumors about him and his sudden penchant for violence. She also heard rumors about what he had done to Katrina Montgomery. In frustration, Merriman ordered her to orally copulate him, and she did until her mouth became sore. Even then he wouldn't relent. This particular assault went on from 11:00 on Saturday night until 10:00 on Sunday night, when he finally allowed her to leave. During this time, she was allowed a break only to go to the bathroom. And even then he escorted her there to make sure she wouldn't sneak out the window.

A few nights later, Andrea Morrow was having a tattoo placed on her derriere when Merriman showed up. He continually slapped her bottom and said, "There, it'll help the ink set."

Andrea Morrow became angry at him, but he didn't back off. Instead, he dragged her into a bathroom and forced her to sit on the toilet. He held her there while he pulled out a hypodermic needle and attempted to inject heroin into his arm. But he kept missing the vein. When he did, he would draw blood out and squirt it in her face. Then he told her, "If you don't watch it, I'll slice your throat like I did to Trina."

Assaulting Sally Crocker, Andrea Morrow, and Sandra Elmwood wasn't enough for Justin Merriman. Since 1996, he had a live-in girlfriend named Wendy Applegate as well. They would often have consensual sex, but just like with the others, she recalled, "He would perform bizarre sexual practices." She said, "He liked to be jerked off while looking at porno magazines." According to Applegate, Justin would even force her to perform this while his male friends were around. If she got "mouthy" about it, he would slap her around.

Wendy Applegate recalled one particular occasion when

both she and Merriman were at Bridget Callahan's house. Callahan was a Skin Head Dogs girl who also believed in their racist creed. Merriman became upset when Applegate ate some cereal that he wanted to eat. He dragged her into the living room and beat her with a belt right in front of Bridget Callahan.

During the whole time Wendy Applegate lived with Justin Merriman, she never knew him to hold down a job. She said he considered himself to be like a male lion. It was up to females to provide for him. His mother certainly did that. She paid for just about everything Justin owned. It was a very strange household on Miller Court in Ventura.

Justin even tried to talk his mother into running a scam for him to get an SSI check. He brought it up while he was once again in jail, this time because of a drug bust. He wrote her, "Mom, what am I going to work on while I'm down this time? A SSI check when I get out of here. That check comes from the government every month and it is usually 700 bucks a month. I want you to help me with the paperwork so I can get it when I get out of here."

He explained how he was going to talk to a "psyche" while he was in jail. He said he would con the man into putting him on some kind of medication that would make him "shuffle around and sleep all day." But in fact he was going to spit the pills into the toilet and just put on an act. "Hey, for 700 bills a month, why not?"

Justin told her he wanted to get things rolling ASAP.

Beverlee Sue wrote back, "We need to discuss this in person with each other. I still have no contact with Caron's office [a local lawyer] about this. With the disability we have to get reports from new doctors and establish your injuries."

Once he was back on the street, Merriman couldn't restrain his violence toward anyone, men or women. On April

16, 1996, he and Scott Porcho were at a club in Santa Barbara that played alternative music. While the band was playing, an altercation broke out between Bret Wittman, a University of California at Santa Barbara student, and some skinheads. Security and Wittman's friends jumped in to break up the fight, and Wittman and the others were escorted toward the door. But as they were, Justin Merriman followed Wittman and punched him in the nose. Wittman fell to the floor, and Scott Porcho kicked him in the head two or three times. Then Porcho and Merriman took off running.

Bret Wittman was taken to the hospital and required thirteen stitches above his right eye. Both Merriman and Porcho were eventually caught. But all they got out of the incident were a couple of misdemeanors. To a man like Justin Merriman, it was a slap on the wrist. After all, he had raped women, used drugs, was in and out of jail, and had murdered Katrina Montgomery, and no one seemed to be doing anything about it. But even as Justin Merriman continued his depredations against women, one man was taking the first steps to bring him down. The man was Ventura County Deputy District Attorney Ron Bamieh.

II
A DEADLY WEB

EIGHT

THE NEW KID IN TOWN

By 1997, Los Angeles County had gotten nowhere with the disappearance of Katrina Montgomery. It was decided to hand the case over to the Ventura County District Attorney's Office, since it was deemed probable that the crime had occurred there. But this was a case that no one wanted to handle. It wasn't just a cold case, it was downright icy. All the leads had drifted off to dead ends, and at every turn people who knew Katrina Montgomery in the Ventura and Oxnard areas were unwilling to talk about her. Especially members of the Skin Head Dogs and those associated with them.

Finally one man with the Ventura County District Attorney's Office decided to take a look at the Montgomery case. He was a young new deputy DA named Ron Bamieh. According to a *Los Angeles Times* article, Deputy District Attorney Bamieh shook his head when he first saw the report on the disappearance of Katrina Montgomery. He told the reporter that he thought at the time, "Why hadn't anybody solved this murder? Unbelievable. This could have been solved right away if police had pressed harder."

But five years had elapsed by the time he got the case. A lot of evidence that could have been obtained easily in 1992 was difficult to recover by 1997. According to Bamieh, he looked over the documents and told Ventura County District Attorney Michael Bradbury, "We can do this. We need some resources and we need some time."

But time and resources were in short supply in those days, and Bamieh was already bogged down in four other major cases. So he took on the Montgomery disappearance as a side project to be worked on in his spare time, late evenings and mornings before regular work.

Ron Bamieh certainly came from an interesting family. His father, Sam Bamieh, was born in Jerusalem, the son of a Catholic Arab father and Jewish mother. Sam had attended grammar school at Egypt's prestigious Victoria College along with classmate Hussein ibn Talal, later known as King Hussein of Jordan. Another classmate was Adnan Khashoggi, the future Saudi arms dealer who got caught up in the Iran-Contra Affair.

Sam Bamieh eventually emigrated to the United States with sixty dollars in his pocket at the age of seventeen. But he was a go-getter and attended Sacramento State University while holding down a job. He earned his M.B.A. there and taught finance at night while putting together a business. During this time, a young man from Saudi Arabia came to visit and stayed with him for three months. The young man was the future Saudi king, King Fahd.

By the early 1970s, Sam Bamieh was putting on financial seminars attended by presidents and vice presidents of corporations. Slowly but surely he assembled the American Intertrade Group, which dealt in real estate and financial consulting. On top of this he sold trucks to Egypt's president Anwar Sadat, as well as building supplies, mechanical equipment, and electronic goods all over the Middle East. By the 1980s the boy who had come to America with sixty dollars in his pocket was a multimillionaire.

Sam Bamieh's life was not without high adventure. According to an article in the *Ventura County Star*, he was held hostage in one of the Saudi royal palaces for one hundred and thirty-three days because they believed he was a spy for the CIA or Israel's secret service, Mossad.

"I never worked for any government, foreign or domestic," Bamieh told reporter T.J. Sullivan. "It was just mental torture. I couldn't eat [properly]. I thought they were going to poison me."

Upon release, Bamieh sued the Saudi royal family for $52 million, and he received an undisclosed amount in reparations.

Even more intriguing was Bamieh's involvement in the Iran-Contra Scandal. Bamieh knew that Adnan Khashoggi, the Saudi arms dealer, was funneling money to the Iranians in exchange for arms for the Contras of Nicaragua, and had ties to the CIA. As he told the reporter, "I was the first one to talk of the Saudi role in Iran-Contra." And when he talked, people listened, including United States senators.

Despite this black mark during Ronald Reagan's presidency, Bamieh has always been a staunch Republican because of their fiscal policies. He counted among his friends President George H. Bush, who invited him to the White House. He was also friends with George Schultz, Gerald Ford, Al Haig, and, surprisingly, even Ronald Reagan.

Into this remarkable household Ron Bamieh was born. He graduated from the University of Southern California and went on to get a law degree at Chicago's Loyola University. He was appointed by President George H. Bush to the Department of Justice in Washington, D.C., where he worked on aviation disaster cases.

But temperamentally Ron Bamieh was cut out for criminal prosecution rather than civil law. He moved back to California and became a member of the Ventura County District Attorney's Office. From 1993 to 1996 he was assigned to the domestic violence/sexual assault unit. His prosecutorial style was so aggressive that he kept subpoenas handy in the glove compartment of his car.

By 1996, Ron Bamieh was ready to move on, and he became the youngest member of the Major Crimes Unit in the Ventura County District Attorney's Office. Less than a year later he took a look at the Katrina Montgomery case. But he already had a couple of other thorny cases to handle, and the Montgomery case would have to stay on the back burner. One of Bamieh's cases concerned forty-year-old Michael Dasher, who had attacked his elderly parents with a machete while on a drug binge. Dasher forced them to kneel and yelled at them, "Pray for your sins at the altar of death!"

Though he didn't cut them badly, he was arrested and faced charges of false imprisonment, elder abuse, and assault with a deadly weapon.

Even more tragic was another case that Bamieh was prosecuting. Seventeen-year-old Juan Flores went to a party in Oxnard with some friends and got into an argument with college student Luis Romero. In an attempt to impress his friends, Flores pulled a gun on Romero and fired. He hit Romero in the chest and killed him almost instantly.

Bamieh said there was no motive in the case other than the fact that Flores was trying to act tough. Bamieh said, "We have a guy who wants to act tough, and he pulls a gun and now he is liable for the consequences. It's sad. It really is."

When Bamieh finally had time to look into the Montgomery case, he went to the Montgomery home in Los Angeles. Katy Montgomery showed him Katrina's room. It was a room frozen in time, as if everything had stopped on November 28, 1992. There were even red hairs from Katrina's head still entwined in one of her hairbrushes. Bamieh was very moved by the experience and promised Katy Montgomery, "We'll get the people that killed your daughter."

He had already surmised that this was much more than just a missing person's case.

Ron Bamieh took home some mugshots of Justin Merriman, Larry Nicassio, and Ryan Bush. He was sure that at least one of them had something to do with Montgomery's disappearance. Stories he'd heard and old documents kept pointing to these three men. As he later told a *Los Angeles Times* reporter, "These people will not remain silent forever. Someone has to have talked."

To help him in his quest for justice, he took on board District Attorney Investigators Mark Volpei and Dennis Fitzgerald. Investigator Volpei had been a sex crimes detective before moving over to the DA's office. He was just as driven as Bamieh. When he was assigned a case, he was like a bulldog that wouldn't let go. When Volpei looked at the photos of the pretty, missing redhead he was just as determined as Bamieh to bring her killer to justice.

While Justin Merriman was raping and abusing women, Ron Bamieh and his team of investigators were starting to build a case against him as the murderer of Katrina Montgomery. It started out slowly, as Bamieh and the investigators gathered details in their spare time away from other cases. After all, Montgomery's disappearance was now almost five years old, and a lot of the details were either half remembered or lost completely. But Investigator Alexander, who also helped out on the case, kept hearing garbled and half-remembered stories from Merriman's friends about the events of November 27–28, 1992. One of the earliest leads originated with John Cundiff, Scott Porcho's housemate, and a young woman named Judy Taylor. One day in 1995, Taylor went to a party and talked to Cundiff about Montgomery's disappearance. Somehow Justin Merriman heard of this conversation and became very angry.

In April 1995, Taylor went to Merriman's house, and Justin met her at the car door. As they walked toward his house, he suddenly balled his hand into a fist and punched her in the face. She began to cry, ran back to the car, and locked herself in. Merriman came to the car door and apologized for the attack, saying that they needed to talk. Eventually she unlocked the door and walked back toward the house with him. But once they got to the door, he began to beat her again. He forced her into his room and told her not to speak to John Cundiff again or say anything about Katrina Montgomery. She promised to keep silent. But in reality she told Investigator Alexander the story of what happened and that Merriman was linked to the murder of Katrina Montgomery.

It was around this time that Investigator Dennis Fitzgerald first spoke with Skin Head Dogs gang member Mike Wozney about what had happened at Scott Porcho's party in 1992. Wozney was one of Merriman's best friends and compatriots in the Skin Head Dogs. Wozney gave some information about the party but would not elaborate about Katrina Montgomery's disappearance. However, bit by bit, his information and that of others kept pointing toward Justin Merriman's residence on Miller Court as the scene of some sort of crime.

On June 9, 1997, Investigator Fitzgerald interviewed Beverlee Sue Merriman at her home, focusing on why she had phoned Judson Mashburn to come over on a Sunday morning to clean her carpets. She once again told the story that he was there to clean up coffee stains on a white rug. She then told Fitzgerald that she'd heard Justin come home in the early morning hours of November 28, 1992. She'd heard some noises in his bedroom; she did not know if he was alone or with someone. As for November 28, 1992, she told Fitzgerald that Justin slept most of the day. When he awoke in the afternoon, he had a terrible hangover. She gave him some medication for his headache. She swore he had not gone anywhere that day.

All through May and June of 1997, the investigators focused on the relationship between Justin Merriman, Ryan Bush, Larry Nicassio, and Katrina Montgomery. With fragmented bits of stories they began to piece together some facts of what had really occurred at Scott Porcho's party on November 27–28, 1992. By now, they were sure that a fight had occurred over Montgomery and not a card game, and that Apryl Porcho had driven Merriman, Nicassio, and Bush to Merriman's house. Later, in the early morning hours of the twenty-eighth, Katrina Montgomery had most likely driven there herself.

In July 1997, Wayne Gibson of the Sylmar Family was reinterviewed at the office of his probation officer. He was told that if he lied during this interview he would be in violation of his probation and sent back to jail. Under this threat, he admitted that what he'd told LAPD investigators in 1992 and 1993 was a lie. He hadn't picked up Ryan Bush and Larry Nicassio in Ventura at Merriman's house, as he'd said previously. Instead, Bush had shown up at Gibson's house on the twenty-eighth and asked to use his pickup truck. And instead of making up this story on his own, as he earlier related, Gibson told investigators that Ryan Bush had told him to lie about going to Ventura. Bush had even given him directions to Merriman's house to make the lie sound more plausible.

Later, in July 1997, Apryl Porcho was interviewed in Maryland. She had divorced Scott Porcho and was now living in that state under a new name. During the interview she said that Justin Merriman was interested in Katrina Montgomery but that Montgomery was just "teasing him." As the evening of the party went on, Katrina had become more and more intoxicated. What happened next Porcho couldn't say because she wasn't there. But she did relate that she'd been involved in an argument with Montgomery about going to Justin Merriman's house. She'd told her it wouldn't be safe there.

Mike Wozney was once again interviewed by investigators in September 1997 at Corcoran State Prison, where he was now serving time. He said he had gone to the party at Porcho's house in 1992 with his girlfriend and Justin Merriman. But he got into a fight with his girlfriend and left the party at 1:00 A.M., depriving both her and Merriman of a ride back to Ventura. He said he'd returned to Porcho's home on the twenty-eighth at about 10:00 A.M. to pick up Ryan Bush and Larry Nicassio to give them a ride back to Sylmar. He was surprised when Scott Porcho told him that Bush and Nicassio had spent the night at Merriman's house. He was even more surprised when Porcho told him that Katrina Montgomery had gone there, as well. Then Wozney dropped a bombshell. He told the investigator, "Porcho said, 'I think those guys killed her.'" This was the first time investigators had heard this comment from any Skin Head Dogs member.

In the summer of 1997, Deputy District Attorney Ron Bamieh wrote, "Investigators decided to take an aggressive approach to the investigation of Ms. Montgomery's [homicide]. It was decided due to the nature of the Skin Head Dogs, the fear in the community surrounding the Skin Head Dogs and other skinheads, and the lack of cooperation witnesses had given to the investigation over the five previous years, that informants, wire taps, undercover operations, and search warrants would be used repeatedly to find the truth."

A grand jury was convened and Ron Bamieh began issuing subpoenas for various law enforcement officers to tell their stories, as well as Skin Head Dogs members who knew Merriman, Nicassio, and Bush.

To shake things up, Ron Bamieh decided to go after Ryan Bush and Larry Nicassio. It was a means to an end. He was using them to get at Justin Merriman, whom he believed was the most culpable for the crime.

Prior to extensive interviews with Bush and Nicassio, Cindy Morales, an ex-girlfriend of Nicassio, was interrogated, and she told investigators that she had spoken with Larry Nicassio about the murder of Katrina Montgomery. Nicassio had told her that he was asleep on the floor of Justin Merriman's bedroom next to Ryan Bush when Merriman began to rape Montgomery. Nicassio also said that he and Bush were too afraid of Merriman to intervene. He told Morales that after raping Montgomery, Justin Merriman killed her. Nicassio admitted that he helped dispose of her body and got rid of the murder weapons, but that he had not killed her. Morales told investigators that Nicassio had told her all of this in December 1992.

A slightly different set of events with Morales was depicted in an article in the *Los Angeles Times*. It said in part, "In November 1997 they wired one of Nicassio's girlfriends and arranged for her to meet him in a Ventura motel room. The plan was for her to get him talking about the murder."

During the sting operation Nicassio reportedly told her, "Don't say a word. Otherwise me and Ryan and Justin are going to go down."

Up until this juncture, authorities only had circumstantial evidence pointing to Justin Merriman as Katrina Montgomery's slayer. But now they finally had a glimpse into what had really happened in the early morning hours of November 28, 1992.

Larry Nicassio was interrogated immediately after Cindy

Morales's interview. He stated that he had not killed Montgomery. When investigators asked him who did, he invoked his right to counsel. Once he had a defense lawyer, Nicassio told them he knew where Montgomery's body was buried and he would tell them if Ryan Bush agreed to talk, as well.

Ryan Bush was interrogated that same evening, but he stuck with the story that he had told LAPD investigators back in 1992 and 1993. He said he didn't know anything about the murder of Katrina Montgomery. He also said he had no idea where her body was buried or that if she was even dead at all.

At this point Cindy Morales was placed in an interview room with Larry Nicassio. The room contained hidden voice and video monitors. Morales told Nicassio that she had already told investigators about the murder and that he ought to cooperate with them.

Nicassio became very upset. "What did you tell them?" he asked.

"I told them everything," she answered.

"You've just ruined my chances to make a deal with the DA's office!" he said. "What difference does it make now whether I tell them today or after I see a lawyer?"

It was decided at this point by Ron Bamieh to arrest Larry Nicassio for the murder of Katrina Montgomery, even though he had little more than circumstantial evidence. And he made an interesting admission. He said, "[We] charged Mr. Nicassio with the murder of Ms. Montgomery. This decision was made because it was believed the evidence against Nicassio established he was present when Ms. Montgomery was killed. The evidence also established that Mr. Nicassio had attempted to establish a false alibi with Mr. Gibson, and that Mr. Nicassio was involved in an altercation with Ms. Montgomery at the party. The decision was made to take Mr. Nicassio through a fitness hearing and a preliminary hearing. At this point of the investigation, the People believed Mr. Nicassio to be liable for the murder and therefore decided to pursue Mr. Nicassio. The People's plan was to attempt to reach an agreement with Mr. Nicassio in order to gain his cooperation. The decision was made to pursue cooperation with Mr. Nicassio because he was only sixteen years of age at the time of the murder. Mr. Nicassio was considered a youngster by both gangs and had a reputation as a follower amongst the Skin Head Dogs and Sylmar Family. [Merriman] was twenty years of age at the time of Ms. Montgomery's murder and had served a prison term. Merriman was the one suspect with a relationship with Ms. Montgomery, and had a history of violence toward Ms. Montgomery. It would be contrary to the culture of a skinhead gang that Mr. Nicassio could have committed the murder of Ms. Montgomery at Merriman's house without his active participation. The People charged Mr. Nicassio based on a belief that the evidence supported his involvement in Ms. Montgomery's murder; and a belief that Mr. Nicassio's culpability was less than that of Mr. Bush.

It was the investigators' belief that the truth of what happened to Ms. Montgomery would not be determined unless one of the suspects cooperated with the investigators. Of the three possible suspects, Mr. Nicassio was chosen because he was the most palpable suspect. It was decided to reach an agreement with him, secure his cooperation, and then attempt to establish the truth of what happened to Ms. Montgomery with his cooperation.

Even though Larry Nicassio and Ryan Bush were in jail on separate charges (Nicassio for alleged murder and Bush for meth possession), Justin Merriman hadn't been arrested for anything yet. But Ron Bamieh and his investigators were sure that he was somehow involved. Investigator Mark Volpei asked for a search warrant of the Merriman residence, stating:

There is probable cause to believe that the property described herein tends to show that a felony has been committed or that a particular person has committed a felony. The residence is a two-story residential condominium, tan in color with a red tile roof. It is trimmed with brown paint with a garage facing the street. The search is to include all rooms, attics, basements and other parts therein, and the surrounding grounds and any garages, storage rooms, and outbuildings. To include all vehicles on or near the property registered to or under the control of Sue [*sic*] Merriman or Justin Merriman. For the following:

1. Human blood.
2. Blood sample from Justin Merriman.
3. Blood sample from Larry Nicassio.
4. Blood sample from Ryan Bush.
5. Fiber samples.
6. Carpet samples.
7. Photographs.
8. Speakers.
9. Furniture.

The search warrant was approved by a superior court judge, and on the night of November 22, 1997, the search and seizure occurred at the Merriman residence, carried out by Investigator Mark Volpei and other officers. During the sweeps, numerous letters were seized from Justin Merriman's room, along with photos depicting gang parties, former girlfriends, and associates. The letters in particular proved Justin Merriman's gang ties to the Skin Head Dogs. They also tied him to Katrina Montgomery.

A second search was ordered for November 25, 1997, and the investigators wrote that they were looking for the following:

1. Black leather purse.
2. Black leather organizer.
3. Black canvass overnight bag.
4. Forest-green bodysuit.
5. Black beaded sweater.
6. Black half boots.
7. Black leather cowboy boots.
8. Silver sculptured heart.
9. Sterling silver earrings.
10. Writings of any kind relating to rape or murder.
11. Newspaper articles of these crimes.

Check registration slips from Beverlee Sue Merriman were also seized from checks written in 1992 and 1993. A particular check written on November 30, 1992, was used to pay Judson Mashburn for cleaning the carpets. Another check dated March 3, 1993, was used for the same purpose.

Some of the most eye-opening items seized were letters between Justin Merriman and his mother. As Ron Bamieh later said, "These letters indicated the [son's] relationship with his mother as being abnormal compared to the traditional mother-son relationship. [Justin Merriman] has no problems with writing about areas of his life that most sons keep private from their mothers. [Justin] also asked his mother in several letters to commit illegal acts on his behalf, help him communicate with other gang members, and consistently do him favors while he was incarcerated. Ms. Merriman in her return letters always agrees to do whatever

[Justin] had asked. Some of the letters between [Justin] and his mother indicate a relationship other than mother and son. The best description of them is they sound like love letters."

As the grand jury listened to more and more information about the Montgomery disappearance, Mike Wozney was still looking at eight months' incarceration for his crime. He was approached by an investigator for the district attorney's office. (Some indications are that it was Mark Volpei). During the interview, Wozney agreed that if he wore a wire (a recording device) while talking to Justin Merriman, and Merriman actually talked about Katrina Montgomery's disappearance, he wouldn't have to serve the eight months. Wozney did state that he would be killed in prison if he was found to be wearing a wire. So the DA's office decided to use Wozney in a "bait car." This would be a vehicle with a recording device wired within the interior, and a video camera, as well. This kind of car was often used to catch auto thieves.

On December 18, 1997, Mike Wozney and Investigator Mark Volpei drove toward Justin Merriman's residence in separate vehicles. A group of undercover cops were also present as backup in case something went wrong. According to Tracy Wilson of the *Los Angeles Times*:

> [Wozney] went to Merriman's condo and persuaded him to take a drive. Merriman looked strung out. His head lolled back, his eyes closed, then he began to talk about the Montgomery investigation, accusing Nicassio of talking to prosecutors.
>
> "Are they going to be able to find the body, dude?" Wozney asked.
>
> "I don't know," Merriman responded.
>
> From his seat in a car parked one hundred yards

away, Bamieh felt that they were getting close. It had been six months. He'd invested countless hours. Finally, Merriman was talking.

Then it fell apart.

Unexpectedly, Merriman picked up the informant's phone and heard a strange voice on the line—Volpei's. He became agitated and started searching the car for a wire. Bamieh's heart raced. Wozney knew that if the situation turned any dicier, all he had to do was say, "It's a bad day," and officers would rush in. They waited. And the informant talked his way out.

For Bamieh and Volpei it was worse than a bad day. They'd spooked the prime suspect, Merriman.

Court papers show a slightly different version of the incident with the bait car. According to court documents, "Mr. Wozney's evening meeting was hampered when a problem with the monitoring equipment was discovered. While he was driving to pick up [Merriman], Mr. Wozney pulled over in order for Investigator Volpei to fix the equipment. When Investigator Volpei approached the 'bait car' the cell phone rang inside the vehicle. Mr. Wozney had given the cell phone [which was also a wire] number to Merriman earlier in the day, and Merriman was now using it to call Mr. Wozney. Mr. Wozney began talking on the cell phone and Investigator Volpei walked up to the car. Merriman heard Investigator Volpei's voice and immediately became agitated on the phone. Mr. Wozney told Merriman that it was his lawyer. Mr. Wozney then told Merriman that he would be right over. Merriman was extremely paranoid. When Mr. Wozney arrived to pick him up, Merriman began frisking Mr. Wozney and then pulled out a razor blade. Mr. Wozney immediately separated from Merriman as Merriman tried to get Mr.

Wozney into the car. Mr. Wozney managed to jump into the bait car and drive away before Merriman could continue his assault."

Whichever way it went down, both Bamieh and Volpei knew that it would be harder to catch Justin Merriman talking about what he had done to Katrina Montgomery from now on.

The next Skin Head Dogs member that the investigators approached to entrap Justin Merriman in a statement of admission was Christopher Bowen. On December 29, 1997, Bowen was arrested by the Ventura Police on a variety of charges that carried a maximum penalty of sixteen years in prison. While talking to Ventura Police detectives, he told them he knew that Justin Merriman had killed Katrina Montgomery.

On December 31, 1997, Investigator Fitzgerald of the DA's office met with Bowen while he was in custody. Bowen was agitated, and he said he knew that Justin Merriman had raped Sally Crocker. Ms. Crocker had told him that on numerous occasions Merriman would break into her apartment and rape her. Then he said that on December 12, 1996, while Sally was at the hospital giving birth to Larry Mason's baby, he [Bowen] had gone to their apartment to get a few things for her. Merriman was at her apartment and high at the time. He and Bowen talked about previous crimes they had committed and the prisons they'd been in. Out of the blue Merriman told him, "I killed a girl named Trina a few years ago." At the time this comment didn't make any sense to Bowen. He didn't know any girl named Trina.

Some time later, Chris Bowen visited Mitch Sutton's tattoo parlor in Reseda. Bowen looked on the wall and saw a photograph of a redheaded girl. When he asked who the girl was, Sutton said that she had once been his girlfriend. She had gone to a party in Oxnard back in '92 and disappeared. Her name was Katrina. Suddenly Chris Bowen knew whom Justin Merriman was talking about.

After the search and seizure at Merriman's house, Justin and his girlfriend, Wendy Applegate, went into hiding. They stayed at friends' homes and in local motels. Much of it was paid for surreptitiously by Beverlee Sue Merriman. But as a new year dawned, Justin Merriman was about to be captured after an incident that no one would forget.

NINE

INCIDENT ON KELLOGG STREET

On January 30, 1998, at 9:00 P.M., sheriff's deputies were working a crime suppression detail on Ventura Avenue. Sergeant Howe and Sergeant Miller were in charge of four other deputies as they patrolled the area, and were riding in an unmarked police car equipped with floodlights on both the passenger and driver's side windows. Even though it was an unmarked car, both Howe and Miller were wearing windbreakers that had the Ventura County Sheriff's logo on it, as well as stars.

While driving on Ventura Avenue, the two sergeants spotted a young man sitting on a bicycle talking on a pay phone at the corner of Ventura Avenue and Ramona Street. As they drove by, Sergeant Howe noticed that the young man stopped talking and rode away on the bike, along with a female companion on another bike. Since the young man's bicycle had no headlamp or rear reflector, and he was riding on the sidewalk, the officer decided to cite him.

Sergeant Howe tried to get the young man to pull over into a gas station on Ventura Avenue. He yelled at the man, "Sheriff's Department, stop!" But the man continued through the gas station lot and Howe yelled again. "Stop, we want to talk to you."

The young man yelled back, "Leave me alone! Fuck you!"

The young man was Justin Merriman.

As Sergeant Howe got out of the car, Merriman turned his bike around and rode back toward Ramona Street, turned east on Ramona, and then onto Poli Street. Sergeant Howe chased Merriman on foot, but he rode away too quickly to catch. Sergeant Howe had, however, seen the suspect's face fairly clearly under the streetlights. He also noticed that the bicycle was dark green.

Meanwhile, Sergeant Miller in the squad car pursued Merriman. As Miller turned on Ramona Street, he saw Merriman up ahead and gunned the motor, pulling ahead of him and actually grabbing Merriman by the shirt. Merriman hopped off his bike and broke away from the officer. He then ran toward a vacant lot.

By this time, Deputy Sheriff Louis Beery had joined the chase and pursued Merriman on foot into the vacant lot, with Sergeant Miller right behind. As they closed in on Merriman, Justin pulled a large revolver from his waistband. Deputy Beery turned on a flashlight and illuminated Merriman with the gun in his hand. But instead of pointing the gun at the officers, Merriman pointed the barrel at his own head. He yelled, "Get away or I'll kill myself!"

The officers froze when they saw the gun, and Officer Beery shouted out, "Gun!" Merriman kept yelling that he would kill himself if they didn't leave him alone, and the officers yelled back to drop the gun. Instead, Merriman took off away from the beam of the flashlight, into darkness, and over a fence at the back of the lot. Both officers pursued him over the fence, but at a respectful distance, aware that Merriman could take a shot at them at any time. Once over the fence, they remained quiet and listened to footsteps heading for Kellogg Street. They heard someone climbing over a chain-link fence and then onto Kellogg.

When the two officers arrived on Kellogg Street they could no longer see the suspect. But they found a scared Hispanic family there who told them they had just seen a man running toward the corner of Kellogg and Poli.

Meanwhile, in the squad car Sergeant Howe encountered Officer Ross Nideffer of the Ventura Police Department, who had been called to the scene. Howe told Nideffer that he was looking for the female on the bike while Miller was looking for the male. Officer Nideffer got back into his car to look for the female, but he'd driven not more than thirty feet when he spotted the male suspect dashing into a home on the 200 block of Kellogg Street.

Officer Nideffer heard the suspect yelling as he pounded on the door of that residence, "Let me in! You gotta let me in. There's cops all over!"

Just as Nideffer stopped his car, the suspect was let into the house.

Justin Merriman went into a residence occupied by a woman named Janet Rail. Ms. Rail lived there with her daughter and three-year-old granddaughter. Merriman had been at the residence most of the day. During the course of the afternoon, his girlfriend, Wendy Applegate, had been seeking Janet Rail's help in leaving him. In fact, Ms. Rail had thrown Merriman out of the house earlier that evening. He had returned later, and got into a verbal and physical altercation with Applegate until Ms. Rail threw him out again.

Once inside the house, at about 9:15 P.M., Merriman told Rail, "The cops are after me." He then ran into the bedroom of the residence and told her, "Don't turn on the lights." He proceeded to take the bedding off the bed and clothes out of her closet, making a barricade around himself while screaming threats at Janet Rail and her granddaughter.

Merriman yelled, "I know my fucking rights! If you know what's best for you, you'll do as I say." The granddaughter was crying throughout the commotion and Merriman became very agitated. He yelled at Ms. Rail, "Tell her to shut up or I'll find a way to shut her up permanently." Then he shouted again, "Don't open the door! I know my rights. They'll have to break in to get a hold of me."

Eventually, Janet Rail grabbed her granddaughter and visiting guest, Jennifer Browkley, and ran out the front door. Merriman did not attempt to stop them. Even though Mrs. Rail never saw a gun in his possession, she did notice that he had something wrapped in a towel and assumed it was a handgun.

There was only one person left in the house with Justin Merriman at this point—Wendy Applegate. And the officers had no idea what he planned to do with her.

By now, Officer Taylor of the Ventura Police Department had arrived on the scene. Along with Officer Nideffer, he set up a perimeter around the house. Taylor attempted to get Merriman to leave the residence by using the public address system on his vehicle. Instead, Merriman began to barricade himself more fully inside the house. Wendy Applegate told later how Merriman was wild-eyed and irrational and talked about going out with a bang. He told her to find him some Draino. He was going to use it to make a homemade bomb.

Officer Taylor knew it was a desperate situation on Kellogg Street, and he asked for help from the Ventura Police Department SWAT team. This wasn't just some small-time affair. Nearly forty officers arrived in the neighborhood while a helicopter with its searchlight hovered overhead. Once the SWAT team arrived, Officer Taylor threw a phone into the house via a back window in an attempt to communicate with Merriman. But instead of talking on the phone,

Taylor could hear him inside the house creating a great deal of noise.

Justin Merriman was doing more than just creating noise. Wendy Applegate said later that he was like a wild man. He threw things around the house, broke dishes and furniture, and pounded on the walls. He absolutely trashed the place. He also took some precautions to protect himself, building barricades with gathered materials and, according to Applegate, collecting towels because he suspected the officers would use tear gas on him at some point. He wet the towels, which he intended to use over his face as a kind of crude gas mask.

After more than an hour of being trapped inside the house with Merriman, Wendy Applegate saw her chance and escaped out the back window while he was running amok inside. A short time after her escape, tear gas was thrown into the house while six SWAT team members waited outside. After several minutes of inhaling the gas, Merriman opened the front door, stuck his head out and breathed deeply, and then went back inside. After about ten more seconds, Merriman did it again, slamming the door behind him each time. Even though Officer Taylor yelled for him to come out, he ignored the officer's demands.

Less than a minute later, Justin Merriman crawled out onto the front porch and the six SWAT team members approached him. But Officer Taylor noticed that Merriman had a knife in his right hand, and yelled at the SWAT team members to back off. He then ordered Officer Dean to shoot Merriman with Arwin. Arwin is a form of nonlethal ammunition, consisting of blocks of wood instead of bullets. At close range it hits a suspect with great force. After being struck with Arwin in the chest, Merriman crawled back into the house.

But the tear gas was too strong in there by now, and Merriman crawled out onto the porch once again. This time it looked to Officer Taylor that Merriman's vision had been impaired. When Merriman thought he heard an officer approaching, he would slash out in that direction with his knife, only to hit empty space. Taylor yelled at Officer Dean to hit the suspect with Arwin once again. But Officer Dean was too close to use it. So Taylor sneaked up behind Merriman and attempted to kick the knife out of his hand. But his foot missed, and instead of kicking the knife, his shoe hit Merriman in the back of the head. Even this blow had no effect on Merriman. He slithered back into the house and slammed the door once again.

Merriman's refuge was short-lived. He staggered back outside and apparently no longer had the knife in his possession. SWAT team members employed a flash-bang device to divert his attention. Once it went it off, Merriman was startled and reached into his jacket pocket. A second device was thrown and Merriman fell to the ground, but soon came back up with his hand in his jacket pocket. All the officers nearby had their weapons drawn, waiting to see if Merriman pulled a pistol or a knife out of his pocket.

Then, in a rush, Officer Brock Avery came up behind Merriman and attempted to grab him. They both fell to the ground and other officers jumped in to restrain Merriman. But he was indeed like a wild man. He struggled upward, began to run, and was tackled by one of the officers right into a tree. Even while he was being handcuffed, he continued to struggle with the officers, all the while trying to reach into his pocket as if he had a weapon there. As he was pulled away, hands restrained by the cuffs, Merriman continued to fight with the officers as he was dragged kicking and screaming out of the area.

Justin Merriman was driven to the Ventura County Medical Center for examination and then taken to the Ventura

County Jail. Once there, Officer Sam Arroyo of the Ventura Police Department examined Merriman to see if he was under the influence of drugs. Officer Arroyo conducted a blood draw from Merriman and determined that his blood tested positive for amphetamines, cocaine, and opiates.

Meanwhile, in the Rail house the officers found a scene of absolute destruction. Merriman had wrecked furniture, pounded holes into walls, and ripped apart fabric. The place looked as if a herd of elephants had stampeded through it. In his rampage, Justin Merriman had caused at least $55,000 worth of damage in the Rail residence. One thing the officers did not find was the gun. It was found neither in Merriman's possession nor in the house.

But Deputy DA Ron Bamieh had something much more important than the gun in his possession. He finally had Justin Merriman behind bars, if not for the murder of Katrina Montgomery, at least for several other serious charges. Merriman would not be going anywhere for a while, and Bamieh's attempts to turn Merriman's former friends and gang members against him began to move into high gear.

TEN

WEARING WIRES

With Justin Merriman now behind bars, Deputy DA Ron Bamieh and his investigators concentrated on unconventional means in the Montgomery case. It was apparent right from the start that Justin Merriman was not going to be forthcoming about Katrina Montgomery's disappearance. To facilitate this, his former friends and gang members would be induced to wear "wires" on Merriman. In most cases this would be on a quid pro quo basis. The DA's office would help them if they helped convict Justin Merriman.

About these tactics Ron Bamieh related in court documents, "Every wire operation conducted by the district attorney's office proceeded in the same manner on every occasion. Prior to commencing an operation with an informant wearing a wire, the informant was told that they were wearing the most sophisticated recording equipment available, that all sounds would be recorded, even the slightest whisper. The informants were told that due to the sophistication of the recording equipment the tapes of their meetings would have to be sent to the Federal Bureau of Investigation for enhancement, and that the district attorney's office would not know exactly what was on the tape until enhancements were completed. Each informant was told that they would be debriefed after each operation and they were to tell the investigator debriefing them everything they could remember from the operation. The informants were told that if they made one mistake between what they told the investigator in their debriefing and what was on the tape that all deals were off and they were on their own.

"In the debriefing, the informants were told if they couldn't remember the conversations exactly they needed to make that clear, never to exaggerate, and to only state as true that which they knew was absolutely correct. All informants were also told never to ask any questions concerning Mr. Merriman's current case [resulting from the incident on January 30, 1998, at Kellogg Street]."

The first person who attempted to sign on board with these tactics was Larry Nicassio. He had very obvious reasons to do so. Nicassio was being charged with a murder he didn't commit and he knew who the real killer was. It had been determined back in November 1997 by Judge Steven Perren that Nicassio would be tried as an adult for the murder of Katrina Montgomery, even though he had been only sixteen years old at the time. Judge Perren stated, "This is because of the seriousness and sophistication of the crime."

In December 1997, after one of Nicassio's court appearances, his lawyer, Darren Kavinoky, had approached Ron Bamieh about making a deal. Kavinoky told Bamieh that his client was innocent of murdering Katrina Montgomery and would cooperate fully with the district attorney's office if Nicassio was not prosecuted for first-degree murder. This deal was rejected by Ron Bamieh, but he kept an open mind about what he would accept and waited for Nicassio and his lawyer to come up with some new offer.

Meanwhile, in February 1998 Skin Head Dogs member Mike Bowman was approached by Ron Bamieh and his investigators. Bowman was serving an eight- to ten-year sentence and agreed to work with them if his sentence was reduced to five years.

On February 5, 1998, Mike Bowman was placed in a "wired" cell along with Justin Merriman at the Ventura County Main Jail. For the next few days, Bowman and Merriman were housed together while Merriman was withdrawing from his heroin addiction and on suicide watch. During this period Merriman often hallucinated and was extremely paranoid. Every time Bowman brought up the subject of Larry Nicassio or Katrina Montgomery, Merriman would become very agitated and point to the ceiling intercom speakers, saying, "Don't mention names."

Once Bowman was taken out of the cell with Merriman and debriefed on February 10, 1998, he told Investigator Volpei that Merriman had talked about his current case without his prompting. Bowman said that Merriman had told him, "I stashed the gun under the kitchen sink" on Kellogg Street. Merriman then went on to say that he had been hiding out in a small room under the kitchen sink just prior to being arrested for the bike incident. But as for the main purpose of the wires, Merriman uttered not a word about the Katrina Montgomery murder. He seemed to have a sixth sense for when to clam up about it.

On March 4, 1998, Mike Bowman was back wearing a wire. He was placed in the Hall of Justice holding tank along with Justin Merriman, where Merriman was being held before his hearing on the Kellogg Street incident. Bowman brought up the name Scott Porcho and Merriman became very angry. Nonetheless, Bowman pursued this line of conversation, saying he had spoken to Larry Nicassio and Scott Porcho recently. Bowman said that he knew the DA's office had approached both of these individuals about making a deal if they could "get" Justin Merriman on the Montgomery murder. Bowman went on to say, "Scott Porcho was brought from prison to Ventura for just that reason. Porcho told investigators, '[Montgomery] left my pad and went to Merriman's house.'"

Merriman responded to Bowman, "Tell Porcho to stop talking to the motherfuckers. All I know is no one's been killed, as far as I know. You know what I mean? That's period." Mike Bowman's attempts to get Merriman to talk about the murder didn't get any further than that.

Meanwhile, Chris Bowen was housed next to Scott Porcho, and he learned that Porcho was passing kites to Merriman, Nicassio, and Bush, telling them that he was going to be wired, so they should watch what they said around him. When Porcho was confronted about this by the investigators he admitted that he had sent the kites, but that he had done it for his own protection rather than trying to tip off the others. Investigator Volpei listened to this story with a grain of salt. Scott Porcho always seemed to tell different versions of "the truth."

Late in February 1998, a local con man, whom the investigators nicknamed John C., sent a letter to Deputy DA Ron Bamieh concerning Merriman. John C. had been arrested on a narcotics charge in January 1998. In the letter he said he could provide information that tied Merriman to the murder of Katrina Montgomery if Bamieh helped him with his own case.

John C. was interviewed at the Ventura County Main Jail. He said he knew Justin Merriman from hanging around Ventura Avenue. He stated that just prior to his arrest he had been in a house buying drugs when he ran into Merriman. Merriman told him, "A homeboy [Larry Nicassio] has been arrested for slicing some girl's throat in '92." But he indicated to John C. that the police had the wrong guy. "I sliced the girl's throat back in '92," Merriman told him. John C.

Katrina Montgomery as a freshman at Saint Bonaventure High School in Ventura, California. *(Yearbook photo)*

...and in her later teen years. *(Photo courtesy of Ventura County Justice Center)*

Justin Merriman and his mother, Beverlee Sue Merriman.
(Photo courtesy of Ventura County Justice Center)

Justin and his Skin Head Dogs buddies.
(Photo courtesy of Ventura County Justice Center)

Justin thought Katrina would be his girlfriend when he got out of prison.
(Photo courtesy of Ventura County Justice Center)

On November 27, 1992, Katrina Montgomery went to a party at Scott and Apryl Porcho's house.
(Photo courtesy of Ventura County Justice Center)

Larry Nicassio was at the party when Justin Merriman handed him a steak knife and told him to "get" Katrina. *(Photo courtesy of Ventura County Justice Center)*

Nicassio

Ryan Bush, Nicassio's cousin, helped pin Katrina up against a wall while Merriman watched. *(Photo courtesy of Ventura County Justice Center)*

Bush

Apryl Porcho warned Katrina not to go to Justin's townhouse. *(Photo courtesy of Ventura County Justice Center)*

Merriman, Nicassio, and Bush placed Katrina's body, wrapped in a blanket, into her pickup and drove it to an area known as Sunset Farms. *(Photo courtesy of Ventura County Justice Center)*

Merriman whipped this handgun out of his waistband
when he was pulled over for a traffic violation.
(Photo courtesy of Ventura County Justice Center)

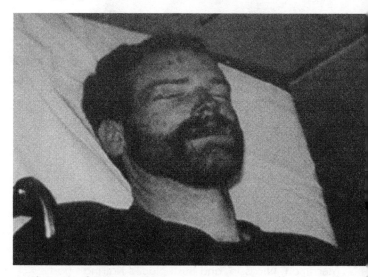

In the jail infirmary, Merriman recovered from injuries inflicted
during a seven-hour standoff in which he held a SWAT team
at bay. *(Photo courtesy of Ventura County Justice Center)*

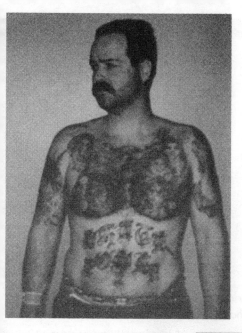

Merriman's numerous tattoos included faces of women, wizards, gang symbols, and the words "White Power."
(Photo courtesy of Ventura County Justice Center)

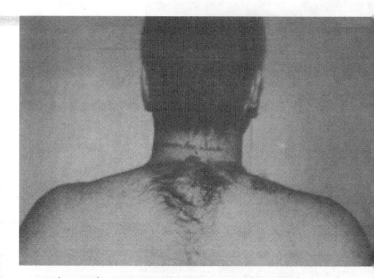

On his neck, Merriman had a tattoo of his mother's name, "Beverlee Sue." *(Photo courtesy of Ventura County Justice Center)*

At the Main Jail Visitor Center, Justin communicated to his network through his mother by writing code words on the glass partition. *(Photo courtesy of Ventura County Justice Center)*

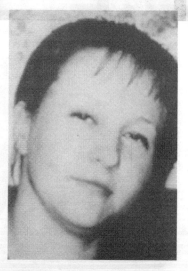

Nicole Hendrix was murdered by Skin Head Dogs members because they thought she was a snitch. *(Photo courtesy of Ventura County Justice Center)*

Michael Bridgeford and David Ziesmer dismembered Hendrix's body, placed it in a garbage can, and filled the can with cement. *(Photo courtesy of Ventura County Justice Center)*

Bridget Callahan went to Saint Bonaventure High School with Katrina Montgomery and attended many Skin Head Dogs parties. *(Yearbook photo)*

Bridget was a key informant, not only in the Nicole Hendrix murder case, but in that of Katrina Montgomery as well. *(Photo courtesy of Ventura County Reporter)*

During the winter of 2001, Judge Vincent O'Neill, Jr.
presided over an emotionally-charged courtroom
in the Justin Merriman murder trial.
(Photo courtesy of Ventura County Star*)*

It took Deputy District Attorney Ron Bamieh, left, with investigator Mark Volpei on right, more than four years to bring Justin Merriman to trial—but he never gave up.
(Photo courtesy of Bryan Chan/Los Angeles Times)

Beverlee Sue Merriman would do almost anything to help her son, including engaging in a conspiracy with him— an act for which she was arrested and served time in jail.
(Photo courtesy of Ventura County Star)

At his trial, Justin flashed gang signs like this letter "W," for White Power. *(Photo courtesy of Ventura County Star)*

Merriman's defense attorney, Willard Wiksell, was clearly disappointed when his client was found guilty of first-degree murder. *(Photo courtesy of* Ventura County Star*)*

After Merriman was found guilty of first-degree murder, Katrina's mother, Katy, thanked co-prosecutor Kevin Drescher. *(Photo courtesy of Ventura County Star)*

Katrina Montgomery's body is buried somewhere beneath this warehouse complex. *(Author's photo)*

said that he would be willing to wear a wire on Merriman at some future time.

As Ron Bamieh was in the process of setting up a deal with John C., Larry Nicassio finally came on board. On March 30, 1998, he and his lawyer reached an agreement with the DA's office. According to Tracy Wilson of the *Los Angeles Times*:

> Nicassio signed an agreement with the District Attorney. He would tell them everything and they would reduce the charge to manslaughter.
>
> "Where is she?" Bamieh asked after Nicassio signed the papers. He had a search team standing by. He wanted to find her body that day.
>
> "We buried her at Sunset Farms," Nicassio answered.
>
> "Tell us what happened," Bamieh said.

Larry Nicassio went through the whole story about the party at Scott Porcho's house in November 1992, and the rape and murder at Justin Merriman's residence. Bamieh didn't believe everything Nicassio was saying, but there were enough facts that did make sense.

Later that day, Nicassio went with the investigators to Sunset Farms, where Ryan Bush had buried Montgomery's body. But since he had been there last the area had totally changed. It was now an industrial park, and with absolute panic Nicassio realized that Montgomery's body was buried somewhere beneath the floor of a warehouse. There was no way he would be able to show the investigators her remains.

Larry Nicassio was so upset by this new development that he sat down and cried. There wasn't going to be any forensic evidence leading straight back to Merriman and clearing him of murder charges. Bamieh told Nicassio, "You're going to have to put on a wire and talk to Justin."

It was back to square one for Ron Bamieh, and the investigators, as well. Instead of mute tangible evidence, they would have to try using informants and recording devices once again, knowing that Justin Merriman was already suspicious because of the failed "bait car" incident, and Scott Porcho's kite to him to beware of people wearing wires.

In April, a new, disturbing wrinkle erupted in the case. On April 18, 1998, Jason Haley was chased by officers through downtown Ventura after a confrontation at the bus station. During the chase, Haley put a pistol to his head and threatened suicide. The officers told him to drop the gun. Instead, Haley turned toward the officers with the gun still pointed at his head. Fearing for their safety, the officers shot and killed Haley.

Within days, Justin Merriman, through his lawyer, claimed it was Haley, not he, who had been on the bicycle back on January 30, and it had been Haley confronted by officers in the empty lot. Merriman said that since he had never threatened them in the first place, there was no probable cause to follow him to the house on Kellogg Street. He wanted all charges dropped and to be released.

While this was being mulled over by the court, Ron Bamieh got John C. to agree to wear a wire on Merriman in exchange for having his sentence dropped to a year in local custody and three years' probation. John C. was placed in the courthouse's holding tank along with Merriman and several other inmates. John C. worked on Merriman with a mixture of truth and lies to see if he could trip him up. He made up part of his tale as he went along. John C. told Merriman, "I hear Nicassio is telling everyone that he didn't kill Katrina Montgomery." This information was meant to shake Merriman up.

But Merriman shot back, "Are you serious? Why is he telling? Tell him to shut the fuck up! So, he's going to give me up?"

John C. added that Nicassio was saying that Merriman had killed Montgomery on his own and not with the help of himself or Ryan Bush.

Merriman replied, "Oh my God, man. I'm going to fucking . . . You should have fucked his ass up. That's a rat. Punch his ass up. Ah, man, get the fuck on him. He's telling you straight out like that? Thump him!"

John C. responded that he did not want to get into trouble over this, but Merriman continued, "Yeah, but he's a rat. You don't break his arm. Just beat him up. Don't say nothing about me. Just tell him I've heard enough of your fucking snitching, you fucking snitch."

John C.: "He's telling me, but I don't know what he's telling everybody."

Merriman: "He's a rat."

John C.: "I guess that article in the paper about them digging up Scott [Porcho's] house over there."

Merriman: "Digging up Scott's house?"

John C.: "Yeah, the backyard. You didn't read about that?"

Merriman: "Uh-uh."

John C.: "Yeah. It was in the paper. Larry came back and said the DA was using his own dog or something. I don't fucking know what's going on."

Merriman: "Oh my God."

John C.: "But it's in the paper. They came out with it in the L.A. *Times.*"

Merriman: "In the L.A. *Times?*"

John C.: "Yeah. Scott and those guys were saying, hey, they dug up my backyard . . . You know him? You know Chris?"

Merriman: "Chris Bowen?"

John C.: "Yeah. 'Cause those guys talk all the time."

Merriman: "Who, Larry and Chris?"

John C.: "Yeah, 'cause they're in twelve and we're in two."

Merriman: "He's supposed to be a rat."

John C.: "That's what I heard, too. But there's no paper-work. So I don't know."

Merriman: "I read all his shit."

John C.: "He and Larry kick it off. I mean, through the vent all the time."

Merriman: "Why?"

John C.: "'Cause they're buddies. [Larry says] if Mumbles would just admit to it, me and my cousin would walk."

Merriman: "He said I'm gonna do whatever it takes to get out of here?"

John C.: "Yeah. He said he's walking. That's when [another prisoner named Mike] said, hey, Larry, you fuckin' piece a . . . Hey, I don't know. I haven't seen the paper-work. But he had a big old fucking envelope he gave his lawyer to mail out. You know he goes to court a lot."

Merriman: "Hey, he told you straight out like that?"

John C.: "Yeah, he was saying it through the vent . . ."

Merriman: "Why didn't you pop him one?"

John C.: "'Cause I'm not ready to get a fucking strike for you guys, homes."

Merriman: "Yeah, but he's a rat. You ain't gotta break his arm, just beat him up a little. Rough him up. Sock him up. And fuckin' tell him to get the fuck out of here."

John C.: "Tell him to move to another section?"

Merriman: "Sock him up first. Sock him in the eye a little."

John C.: "He drives me . . . All he does is paperwork. Boom, boom, boom. From what I understand, he told. Everybody says they know it. Chris, Scott, all the guys. 'Cause I guess he wants, what do you call it . . . for-giveness."

Merriman: "He wanted forgiveness?"

John C.: "Yeah, 'cause the way he looks at it, he didn't

do anything . . . so he thought he'd ask forgiveness of the family."

Merriman: "Why the fuck did he say anything? Oh, man."

John C.: "He keeps saying, 'I didn't do it.' He's like quote, unquote, 'Justin would admit to it. Then me and my cousin could walk.' "

Merriman: "What did you do?"

John C.: "I just told him to shut up. I told him to shut his mouth. I don't want any of this bullshit."

Merriman: "Ahh, but come on, man. Touch him up. Tell him to push that button to get the fuck out now."

John C.: "He's walking. So they're getting him first, and, uh, once they got him, they're going to come get you guys. But if he ends up giving up the body, he's walking. He's already looking at brand-new cars in the paper and shit like that."

Merriman: "Are you serious?"

John C.: "Yeah. He goes, I want a new car and this and that. He said there is reward money, too."

This outburst by Merriman was definitely a threat against another inmate, but still Justin Merriman had not decisively indicated that he was directly responsible for Montgomery's murder.

Meanwhile, Ryan Bush was yelling from a nearby holding tank during this whole exchange, and Merriman yelled back to Bush, "Hey, your cousin is going to rat. He told [John C.] everything, dog. He said you and him are gone in a year. He'll do whatever it takes to get out of here. Told your grandparents everything. Hey, is it just him or what? His cellie right here, told everything. Says you two are gonna walk in a year."

Bush denied that he had anything to do with this. But he said he couldn't speak for Nicassio.

After this episode, Ron Bamieh and his investigators knew that other gang members would not feel comfortable talking to or being around Larry Nicassio. So they cooked up a scheme to make it seem that Nicassio was being lied about in his cooperation with the authorities. They filed a false fitness report on Nicassio, stating that he was not co-operating at all, and made this finding general knowledge. Even Justin Merriman heard about it.

On April 22, 1998, a wire was rigged on Larry Nicassio and he was placed in the same holding tank with Merriman at the courthouse. Merriman and Nicassio exchanged a few heated words, but then Nicassio let him read the false report about his so-called noncooperation and Merriman cooled down.

As Nicassio began to talk again, Merriman became angry when Nicassio raised his voice above a whisper, and told him to keep his voice down.

Nicassio said to Merriman that he'd told his lawyer everything about the murder. Merriman responded, "That's not good."

Then Merriman offered to pay Nicassio's lawyer's fees as long as he took the rap for the murder. Merriman wanted to know who had said that he'd raped Montgomery. He also said, "Don't worry about Judson Mashburn and the cleaned carpets or John Cundiff and all the stuff he's been saying. I've beaten up Cundiff a couple of times and the guy is afraid of me."

Unfortunately, the quality of the sound on the recording device was very poor because of the background noise in the holding tank. There were more than a dozen inmates in the tank at that time, and music in the background interfered with the recording. And even more unfortunate that this was the fact that, once again, Justin Merriman uttered not a word that would clearly implicate him in the murder of Katrina Montgomery.

* * *

Finally Merriman told Nicassio that he would arrange a "hookup" with him at visiting time so that they might talk more freely. Merriman would arrange it so that a visitor came in to see Nicassio while he had a visitor at the same time. They'd be able to sit side by side and discuss things more easily.

Bits and pieces of the story were coming in from all directions to Investigator Volpei at this point. He received a phone call from a young woman who had helped him as an informant on another case in the past. She told him that she had been in rehab with a girl named Andrea Morrow. Morrow had told the informant that Justin Merriman had raped her in Ventura some years before.

Investigator Volpei set it up so that the young woman wore a wire while talking to Andrea Morrow. On the recording device, Morrow's voice clearly mentioned that Justin Merriman had once told her that he had sliced Katrina Montgomery's throat with a knife.

All of this was good, but so far it was just hearsay. The investigators wanted to hear the admission coming from Merriman's own lips, so the wires continued. On May 18, 1998, Andrea Morrow agreed to wear a wire on Justin Merriman. She phoned the Merriman residence and left a message on the answering machine saying that she wanted to see Justin. The next day she contacted Beverlee Sue Merriman and asked to meet her at the local coffee shop. Beverlee Sue agreed.

Andrea Morrow was wearing a wire when Beverlee Sue arrived. Both Investigators Volpei and Fitzgerald were waiting outside and saw Beverlee Sue Merriman enter the establishment. She talked with Morrow for nearly a half hour. When Beverlee Sue left, the investigators debriefed

Morrow and she told them what the other woman had said. Beverlee Sue told Morrow that back on November 28, 1992, Larry Nicassio, Ryan Bush, Justin, and Katrina Montgomery had indeed all been at her house. But she lied to Morrow and said that she'd watched Montgomery leave of her own accord later that morning and was never seen again.

The conversation turned back to Nicassio. Beverlee Sue said that Justin was very upset about Nicassio. She asked if Morrow would come in to visit Nicassio at the same time that she went to visit her son. Andrea Morrow agreed to go along with her.

This worked well as far as the investigators' own schemes went. On May 20, 1998, they wired Andrea Morrow once again and had her accompany Beverlee Sue Merriman to the main jail. Unknown to Morrow, Larry Nicassio was wearing a wire, as well. Neither Nicassio nor Morrow knew that the other one was wired.

It was by now a strange game of cat and mouse between the suspect, Justin Merriman, and the investigators, Volpei and Fitzgerald. Each was trying to outwit the other on the Montgomery murder. Since Andrea Morrow didn't know Larry Nicassio, Beverlee Sue Merriman had to describe his appearance and instructed her what to do if she was ever contacted by the police. Of course, Beverlee Sue had no idea that Morrow was wearing a wire while she said this. Then the two women went into the visiting room where they were met by Nicassio and Justin Merriman on the other side of the screen.

Justin Merriman thanked Andrea for coming and introduced her to Nicassio. Merriman spoke to his mom for a short time, while Morrow spoke to Nicassio. Finally they got down to the real business at hand. Justin Merriman told Nicassio, "Tell your lawyer to provide you with all the paperwork on the Montgomery murder." Nicassio was then to pass these documents on to him. By this means, Merriman could find out just who was talking behind his back.

Both Nicassio and Morrow must have had a bad moment about this. Both of them were mentioned in the paperwork as wearing wires, along with John C., Mike Bowman, Chris Bowen, and Scott Porcho.

Justin Merriman then told Nicassio he was concerned about some of the blood found in his room. He said, "Most of that blood was my blood from slammin' dope. But some of that blood was her blood."

He said that money was coming to Nicassio's aid and not to talk to or cooperate with the DA's office. He argued that Nicassio could recant anything he said in the past that tied Merriman with the murder. And as far as Katrina Montgomery's body went, "If that shit comes out of the ground, we'll be in L.A. County."

On May 28, a similar four-way meeting was arranged at visiting hour, with Nicassio and Morrow wearing wires unbeknownst to the other two. At this time Nicassio asked Merriman, "Was the blood in the room cleaned up well?" Justin Merriman nodded yes, and said, "Don't worry about any blood found in the truck. We can say Katrina was on the rag. Me and her could have had sex in the back of that truck for all they know."

On June 3, 1998, another one of these meetings was arranged, but Justin Merriman was becoming more suspicious. He didn't like the stories he was hearing about Nicassio and he was worried about Andrea Morrow, as well. He told his mother that he didn't want Morrow coming to the jail anymore and totally clammed up.

To jump-start the investigation, which had hit a snag, Andrea Morrow was instructed to phone Beverlee Sue Merriman with the story that she felt Larry Nicassio was feeling alone and desperate and that he was considering talking to the DA's office with some very damaging evidence. She made this phone call on August 10, 1998, and Beverlee Sue agreed to meet with her at the coffee shop again. Just like the previous time, Andrea Morrow wore a wire.

When Morrow spoke to Beverlee Sue Merriman she related just how despondent Nicassio had become. She said he was all alone out there, taking the heat. In response, Beverlee Sue Merriman answered that all of Nicassio's mail at the jail was being read and he should be careful what he said. Just how she knew this fact, she didn't say.

Andrea Morrow met Beverlee Sue again on August 16, 1998, with a letter that had been crafted by Ron Bamieh and his investigators, with the permission of Larry Nicassio's lawyer. It purported to be a letter from Darren Kavinoky to Nicassio, asking for more money because Katrina Montgomery's body had been found and the case was moving to Los Angeles County. All of this, of course, was a fabrication.

On September 11, 1998, Justin Merriman sent Nicassio a kite saying he was trying to arrange another four-way meeting at the visitors' area. That same day Andrea Morrow and Beverlee Sue Merriman arrived for the meeting, and Morrow was wired as usual. Nicassio was, as well. Nicassio had a few tricks up his sleeve to try and trick Merriman into making an admission. One was that his lawyer had told him Katrina Montgomery's body had indeed been found, and that there was evidence that led directly back to Justin Merriman's house. The other was that if Nicassio went to trial, he was going to admit that Montgomery had been at the Merriman residence before disappearing. Nicassio raised his voice above a whisper and told Justin, "L.A. County has got the body."

Merriman responded, "Oh my God! That's another trick. Don't believe that shit! I think your lawyer is playing you.

There's no need to be trippin'. [Your lawyer] has got these fuckin' Christian deals, whatever."

Nicassio: "He can't fuckin' play me like that."

Merriman: "Hey, I'm telling you they would have already charged me if [unintelligible]. He's playing you. I guarantee it."

Nicassio: "He's my lawyer. He ain't gonna fuckin' tell me no shit like that."

Merriman: "Remember what I told you. Don't tell him nothin'."

Nicassio: "Hey, he told me [Montgomery] showed up at your pad."

Merriman: "No, no, no. I don't even know what you're talkin' about, dog."

Nicassio: "My lawyer ain't gonna lie to me, homes."

Merriman: "Shhh. Shut the fuck up."

Nicassio: "Look, if I go to L.A.—"

Merriman: "Shhh. Don't do nothin' your lawyer said."

Nicassio: "But if I go to L.A. I'm going to come out with, she came to the pad."

Merriman: "Hey! Don't make a fuckin' statement at all. I swear to God. If you fuckin' . . . That's it, dog."

Nicassio: "If I go to trial what am I goin' to say?"

Merriman: "If you say one more thing out loud like that again, I'm going to bust you in the eye. Listen to me, man. Quit fucking being loud. Are you wearing a wire?"

Nicassio: "You wanna check me out?"

Merriman: "You listen to me, man. Come here. Don't make a statement at all."

Nicassio: "I'm talking about a trial."

Merriman: "We'll worry about it when we get there. Look, if you don't keep your motherfucking voice down I'm gonna . . . If you make a statement she was there and left, that brings her blood and me right into it. Do not make that fucking statement. That will drag me and Ryan into it."

Nicassio: "If they find that shit . . ."

Merriman: "Hey, man, come here. Check it out, brother. I'm being serious as a fuckin' heart attack. Your fuckin' lawyer is fucking with you. This shit is getting old. My lawyer is out there. He knows a lot of people in this county. They got a mountain of wood. They don't have shit."

Nicassio: "Well, but what about me?"

Merriman: "I'm tellin' you, your lawyer has them Christian ethics."

Nicassio: "Listen to me. If my lawyer says okay, I got to admit to her being at the pad."

Merriman: "No, no."

Nicassio: "And she left and we never seen her again."

Merriman: "What? Why?"

Nicassio: "If they come up on that shit, they'll have proof that she was there. I'm telling you I ain't no fucking lame. If I go to trial, I'll have to admit to her being there, okay?"

Merriman: "If you do that, you're dragging me into a mess. What are you fucking thinking? Why would you do that? You could have just went to the fuckin' store, getting beer with her. Why drag her to my fucking pad? You're dragging me in. Why would you do that?"

Nicassio: "If they find my or your hairs . . ."

Merriman: "Look. You took her to the fuckin' store, you kissed her, I don't give a fuck what you say. But you can't have her coming to my pad. Do not go there!"

Justin Merriman was just paranoid enough and cagey enough to never quite admit that he had anything to do with

Katrina Montgomery's murder. Despite all the prodding by people wearing wires on him, Justin Merriman skated across their snares like an expert ice skater. Not once did he say, "I killed her." He may have told people in the past that he did, but that was all hearsay. Not one word of it crossed his own lips and onto a recording device. He seemed to have nine lives as far as the wires went.

But as October 1998 rolled around, Justin Merriman was not Ron Bamieh's only Ventura skinhead problem. In that month, some of Justin Merriman's Skin Head Dogs friends had just murdered another girl in the most brutal fashion imaginable.

ELEVEN

THE GIRL IN THE
BARREL OF CEMENT

Bridget Callahan was a Skin Head Dogs girl and close
friend of Justin Merriman. Bridget had been a pretty girl at
St. Bonaventure High School in Ventura. She was a few
years older than Katrina Montgomery, who had also attended classes there. Because of Bridget's small stature, she
had the nicknames of "Smidget" and "Small Stuff." Callahan was very bright and a member of various school
organizations. But just like Katrina Montgomery, she, too,
liked to walk on the wild side. She constantly hung out with
Skin Head Dogs members, and according to one source was
an on-again, off-again girlfriend of Skin Head Dogs member David Ziesmer. Some said that, much more than Katrina
Montgomery, Bridget believed in all the white power
rhetoric of her associates. She liked to "mouth off" with
neo-Nazi and gang slang.

During Justin Merriman's incarceration, Callahan
drummed up support for him among other gang members.
She had also been a go-between on visits to him in jail, send-
ing messages to skinheads on the outside. Some of these
bordered on the edges of witness tampering and conspiracy.

Among her closest relations in the Skin Head Dogs were David Ziesmer, twenty-six, and Michael Bridgeford, twenty-three. These two were literally walking billboards for neo-Nazi racism. They were covered with tattoos that proclaimed their hatred of "lesser peoples" and the superiority of the white race. Ziesmer had "88" tattooed on his cheek. Since *H* is the eighth letter in the alphabet, each *H* stood for "Heil Hitler." Above his eyes was the tattoo "Racial loyalty." There were various swastikas tattooed all over his body, and he was a walking, talking billboard of hate.

Since the age of fifteen, Ziesmer had been in jail except for a brief period of six months of freedom. During his incarceration, he had been placed in jails for theft, as well as a myriad of other crimes and parole violations. He told a *Ventura County Star* reporter that his racial beliefs were reinforced at the California Youth Authority and prisons.

Lt. Quinn Fenwick of the Ventura Police Department said about Ziesmer and his friends, "They're very violent. They don't have a coherent philosophy and they victimize people of all races. They have no respect for anybody or anything."

If David Ziesmer had a philosophy at all, it was a hatred of people of color, whom he termed "inferior races" and the "mud people." His Web page on the Internet attested to that. It portrayed a shirtless Ziesmer and Bridgeford linked arm in arm and showing off their tattoos. They went by the Internet names of "Dopey" and "Demon." Under the Web page photo was written "Die Hunde," a loose German translation of their gang's name. They also had Web page links to pen pal addresses of various Aryan Brothers and a guest sign-in book that requested support for their brother in jail, Mumbles (Justin Merriman's gang name).

Michael Bridgeford was just as violent as Ziesmer. On September 10, 1994, he and other gang members attacked twenty-one-year-old Jason Rosseau outside the Metro Bay

Club in Ventura. They chased him down and stabbed him and beat him with clubs. Aside from Bridgeford, the attackers included Jeffrey Newton and Scott Porcho. Even Apryl Porcho had been present, cited, and released. For his part, Scott Porcho was held on $50,000 bail and an eventual trip back to jail. Bridgeford got a stint of several years in state prison.

By 1998, one girl who occasionally hung out with Ziesmer, Bridgeford, and Callahan, and did drugs with them, was seventeen-year-old Nicole Hendrix. (Also spelled Nichole in some records.) She was a habitual runaway who often lived with friends or on the streets around Ventura. She liked to drink and do drugs. And even though she was only seventeen years old, she had a thirty-five-year-old boyfriend. Her mother was very worried about Nicole, especially her truancy and drug use. At one point she even followed her daughter to school every day, just to make sure she attended. It got so bad that eventually Nicole agreed to enter a drug rehabilitation program in Arizona, at her mother's insistence.

On the night of October 14, 1998, Hendrix and some others affiliated with the Skin Head Dogs were arrested for drug-related offenses. After she was arrested, Nicole Hendrix was released into the custody of her mother because of her age. Her mother told her, "Nikki, something bad is going to happen to you if you don't straighten up."

It didn't take long for the "bad thing" to happen. The others who had been arrested, especially David Ziesmer, thought that Hendrix had been released because she had squealed on the others and was a police informant.

Nicole Hendrix didn't know the others thought she was a rat. In fact, the day after she was released she attempted to sell stolen goods from her boyfriend's truck to help raise bail money for the others. She phoned Bridget Callahan to help her sell the items. But before long, Callahan had Hendrix so full of drugs that she passed out.

Callahan, Ziesmer, and Bridgeford, who were now out of custody, decided to take the stolen goods to the City Center Motel in Ventura and sell them from a room. They dragged Nicole Hendrix along with them. Ziesmer was still so incensed at Hendrix that he punched her a couple of times on the way over, spat on her, and called her a rat. Once in the motel room, they attempted to force more drugs on Hendrix, but were unsuccessful. So they dumped her in the motel closet where she passed out once again.

With Hendrix unconscious in the closet, friends of Ziesmer came into the room throughout the day and night to buy stolen goods. When Hendrix recovered from her drugged state, dazed and disoriented, it was a little after midnight on October 16, 1998, and Ziesmer and Bridgeford were out of the room. She phoned her mother from the motel phone and said that she was on her way home. She was so disoriented that she told her mother, "I don't know where I am. Leave the front gate or side gate open and I'll be home."

But her phone call was very badly timed. David Ziesmer walked into the room while she was on the line and was sure that Hendrix was contacting the police. He demanded to know whom she had called, and when she told him it was her mother, he didn't believe her.

"You're a rat!" he yelled, and grabbed her arm.

"No, I'm not!" she countered. "I've never ratted on nobody. Let me go home."

Callahan and Bridgeford, who were also in the room, witnessed this. But they weren't sympathetic with Hendrix's plight, since they believed she was a rat, as well. Ziesmer told them, "She has to go."

Ziesmer forced Nicole Hendrix into the bathroom while he

decided what to do with her. He was just coming down from a four-day methamphetamine binge and very paranoid. He was also suffering from the delusion that he was a three-strike candidate if Hendrix ratted on him about drug use, and would be going back to prison for life. He was wrong in this belief.

As he said later, "At that point in time, I made up my mind to murder Nicole."

Ziesmer told Michael Bridgeford and Bridget Callahan about what he intended to do. Rather than being stunned by this information, Callahan walked into the bathroom and explained to Nicole Hendrix that she was going to have to die. She told her in a very matter-of-fact and unemotional way. As Callahan said later, "She was crying and I gave her a hug and I kissed her on the head and I told her I was really sorry, but there was nothing I could do for her at that point."

In one version, Callahan left the room to guard the front door. In another she turned up the music and stared out the window. David Ziesmer and Michael Bridgeford entered the bathroom. Ziesmer had a Swiss Army knife that he had stolen from Hendrix's purse and a heavy flashlight. While Hendrix cried and begged for her life, the two men placed her in the bathtub.

Ziesmer at first tried to calm her down. She was crying and squirming around in the tub and he wanted an easy target. Once he had her in a good position, Ziesmer struck her with a surprise blow. As he recalled later, "I tried to stab her in the neck first. She didn't see it coming. The knife hit her squarely in the neck and blood spurted out."

Ziesmer recounted, "I continued to stab her in the chest and the neck, and at that time she was getting too wild for me, trying to kick me."

In fact, Hendrix was fighting for her life with every ounce of energy she had. Bridgeford moved in to hold her down and in one version beat her with the heavy flashlight as she struggled. She squirmed and fought back, desperately trying to save her life.

Ziesmer continued, "I was losing it. I kept stabbing, I can't remember where, and I lost the knife in the tub. I pushed Michael out of the way, and I started stomping her on her head area."

As she thrashed around in the tub, trying to stave off his blows, Ziesmer kept on booting her. He was like a wild animal as he jumped on Hendrix's head and kicked in her skull. As his boots slammed into her head and her blood flowed, she became weaker and weaker in her efforts to stop him. Finally she stopped moving.

In fact, she was dead. By the time they were through with Nicole Hendrix she was not only dead, but a complete bloody mess, and so was the entire bathroom.

Afterward, Ziesmer and Bridgeford taped up Hendrix's wounds with duct tape to try and stop the flow of blood, and Callahan helped them roll the body into sheets. Then they all cleaned up the bathroom. But they were continually interrupted by more friends dropping by to purchase stolen goods. Ziesmer conducted business with these people in another room as if nothing had happened. None of those present were aware that there was a dead girl in the bathroom.

After several hours, Ziesmer, Bridgeford, and Callahan managed to clean up the bathroom and main room as best they could, and wrapped Nicole Hendrix's body in a sheet from the motel bed. They dumped the sheet-wrapped body in the back of a pickup during the early hours of the morning. But their next move was so brazen it bordered on madness. The trio drove to Santa Barbara to score some heroin, even while Hendrix's body remained in the back of the pickup. They drove around visiting friends and going to fast food restaurants, all while the sheet-wrapped body of Nicole Hendrix lay in the back of the pickup.

Finally, on October 17 they stopped and bought a large trash can, some cement mix, and, according to one source, a long power cord and chain saw. In the backyard of a friend's house in Oxnard they stuffed Nicole Hendrix's butchered body in the trash can and poured in the wet cement mix over her. But the cement mix never really hardened and Hendrix's body floated in a kind of slurry.

Unconcerned about the body, half congealed in a gumbo of cement, the trio went on a heroin binge while the trash can sat in open sight in a backyard. Even after they came off the binge, Ziesmer and Bridgeford were not individuals who lay low. They assaulted a black man on Ventura Avenue, merely because of the color of his skin. But this time they weren't lucky. They were caught, arrested, and placed in jail.

From jail Ziesmer sent Bridget Callahan a message, "Get rid of the body."

He also phoned fellow gang member James Daniel Bowman and asked him to get rid of the trash can and Hendrix's body.

James Bowman and Bridget Callahan contacted a friend named Roy Ashlock and asked if he could help them get rid of some illegal guns that they had in a trash can. Ashlock agreed, and they all drove up into the mountains on Route 33 to get rid of the trash can. According to most sources, Ashlock didn't know he was helping them dispose of a body rather than illegal guns.

They drove up to Pine Mountain north of Ojai, up twisting Highway 33. There in the realm of the giant California condor they dropped the can over a cliff and down a ravine. There it stayed for the next six months, out of sight, while the participants and the murders of Nicole Hendrix and Katrina Montgomery became incredibly intertwined.

As the days lengthened and Nicole did not come home, her mother paged her constantly with no response. She phoned the police department and sheriff's department seeking any information they might have about her missing daughter. But in this regard she came up empty. She was afraid to leave the house just in case her daughter might phone, or someone else would, with news about Nicole.

Finally, driven to desperation, Mrs. Holland (Nicole's mother) began searching roadside ditches and drug-infested neighborhoods looking for Nicole. She later told a *Los Angeles Times* reporter, "I did some crazy things. But I don't think what I did was any different from what any other parent would do."

Her search included calling morgues in seven different states and Mexico. She knocked on the doors of complete strangers' homes asking if they'd seen her daughter. But what she received was a wall of complete silence, especially from associates of the Skin Head Dogs. This shroud of silence settled over Nicole Hendrix's disappearance just as tightly as the one that had surrounded the disappearance of Katrina Montgomery nearly six years before.

TWELVE

INDICTMENT

Over time, Bridget Callahan became the link between the two unsolved murders. But none of this was evident to Ron Bamieh or his investigators at first. During the fall of 1998 and winter of 1999, Callahan did all she could to find out who among the Skin Head Dogs members was talking to Ron Bamieh and his investigators about Justin Merriman and the murder of Katrina Montgomery, while keeping quiet about the murder of Nicole Hendrix. In fact, she was trying to find out just as much about what Bamieh, Volpei, and Fitzgerald were doing as they were trying to discern what the Skin Head Dogs were covering up and what Callahan's role was. In this twisted labyrinth of intrigue, Ron Bamieh and Investigator Volpei decided to drop by Callahan's apartment in November 1998, not really certain yet where she fit in the mix, but certain that she was a player.

According to Kelly Davis, a reporter for the *VC Reporter*, "[Bridget] seemed nervous but agreed to talk. They scheduled a meeting, but Callahan disappeared before it took place. Volpei later found her abandoned car in a Target parking lot, leading them to wonder if Merriman, who was orchestrating a witness-eradication program from his jail cell, somehow got to Callahan before they did."

During November, various colleagues and family members of Justin Merriman were being hauled before a grand jury by Bamieh. Many of them were unwilling participants, and a few of them were lying to the grand jury, including Justin Merriman's mother, Beverlee Sue Merriman. During these proceedings an article appeared in the *Ventura County Star* regarding Merriman's potential indictment in connection with Montgomery's murder. Shane Matthews, a deputy sheriff in Ventura, phoned the DA's office and spoke with Investigator Volpei. Matthews told Volpei that he was a friend of a woman who knew Justin Merriman's sister, Ember, and the woman had just read the article in the newspaper about Justin. Matthews related that this friend had been told by Ember five years earlier that Justin might be involved in a murder. The woman friend didn't know who the victim was and didn't come forward with this story. But after the *Ventura County Star* article came out about the indictment, she put two and two together and surmised the person Ember Merriman had been talking about must have been Katrina Montgomery.

This woman finally had a get-together with Ember during a church activity called "Accountability." During a session, Ember Merriman told the woman of a morning in November 1992 when she and her mother had cleaned up bloodstains in their house. Ember had asked Justin where the blood came from. He responded, "You don't want to know. I'm going to hell for what I did."

The next day, November 29, 1992, an officer from the LAPD had dropped by the house asking about Katrina Montgomery. Her mother said the blood was from Justin Merriman. But from that point onward, Ember believed the blood was really Katrina Montgomery's.

This woman asked Ember where Justin was that morning while she and her mother were cleaning blood off the stairs.

Ember said that he had gone for a long ride and did not come back for hours. This fact was in direct contradiction to the story her mother had been telling the police and now was telling a grand jury.

With the participation of Investigator Volpei, the woman agreed to make a "cool call" to Ember, who was now married and called Ember Wyman. The woman asked Ember to meet her the next day at her house and Ember agreed. The woman allowed the DA's office to plant a recording device at her home, and Ember Wyman dropped by as planned on November 19, 1998.

During the conversation the woman began talking about the recent article in the newspaper. Ember said she was very nervous about what she knew. And then she said she had lied during her testimony at the grand jury hearing and she was afraid for herself and her mother. She said that her mother had also lied to the grand jury.

Ron Bamieh immediately pounced on this chink in the armor of Justin Merriman's "home defense." Faced with obstruction of justice and perjury, on November 23, 1998, Ember Wyman agreed to tell Bamieh and Investigator Volpei the entire truth of what she knew about the events of November 28, 1992, in exchange for immunity from prosecution. Ember said that on that date she lived with her mother and brother on Miller Court in Ventura. She stated that she did not witness the rape and murder of Katrina Montgomery. Her bedroom was approximately one hundred feet from her brother's room, with three doors separating the rooms. She did not hear any sounds of a struggle.

When she woke up that morning she found her mother scrubbing blood off the stairs that led from Justin's room to the main part of the house. Her mother told her it was Justin's blood from a fight the previous night.

However, in 1992, Ember was engaged to a man named

Jeremy Rice and she told him that she suspected something terrible had happened in her home. She said that when she had confronted Justin about the disappearance of Katrina Montgomery, he wouldn't tell her what happened other than to say, "I'm going to hell for sure."

By November and December 1998, Ron Bamieh had enough evidence against Justin Merriman to keep rolling through grand jury testimony. He brought in Scott Porcho to testify, and Porcho began his "umpteenth" version of the party on November 27–28, 1992. His story always seemed to change in small but important details. Bamieh's questions and Porcho's answers got down to the nitty-gritty of what had really happened there that night.

Q. "I'm speaking of [an incident], one involving Trina in your bedroom. Do you know what I'm talking about?"

A. "Apryl and I were talking, and every once in a while it seems we'd meet up to make sure everything is okay. 'Did you see anything?' What you do at a party. 'Anything get broken?' And we were standing there talking. I think we were in the hallway. And we heard a girl scream, and we both ran towards my bedroom where it seemed the scream came from. And the door was closed, and I just rushed in, and Trina was lying on the bed holding her stomach. Looked like somebody had hit her in the stomach, and there was about eight guys standing in a semicircle around her. And they were looking—they looked aggressive, as in, like, they were getting in a fight."

Q. "Do you remember who those eight people were or any of those eight people?"

A. "Justin was one of them. Justin Merriman. And all of the rest of them were from Sylmar."

Q. "Was Larry [Nicassio] in there? Do you remember?"

A. "I can't be sure."

Q. "How about Ryan Bush?"

A. "I can't be sure. There's only one guy I remember in particular because he seemed the most aggressive of all of 'em, and I can't remember his name."

Q. "And you do remember Justin being there?"

A. "Yes, because he's the only one I spoke to."

Q. "And what did you say to him?"

A. "I said, 'What's going on?' "

Q. "And what was his response?"

A. "Nothing."

Q. "And did you clear the room?"

A. "Apryl picked up Trina and walked her out of the room, and all the guys from Sylmar kind of slowly trickled out. And I'm going, 'What's going on?' [Merriman] goes, "Nothin's going on.' I go, 'You sure nothin's going on?' He goes, 'Nothing.' And I was looking at him, angry. And he's saying nothing happened. I go, 'Okay,' and I walked out."

Q. "Now, did you see an incident involving Justin and Trina again that evening?"

A. "Yes."

Q. "Where did that occur?"

A. "In the hallway. Can I point it out?"

Q. "Sure."

A. [Pointing to a diagram] "Right here, the top of the hallway, right where the kitchen intersects with it."

Q. "Okay. So you pointed to the area of the hallway on that diagram. Upper hallway. We're talking A.M. or still in the P.M.?"

A. "Yeah, A.M. It was probably around one or two, maybe

even three, I know it was very late. There were very few people left there."

Q. "What did you see going on?"

A. "I saw Trina backed up against that wall, right here. [Pointing to diagram] I was sitting in the kitchen at the table with John Cundiff, and he said, 'Scott, look.' And I followed his arm pointing towards the hallway. And Trina's back was against the wall right there, and Larry was choking her with two hands."

Q. "Larry Nicassio?"

A. "Larry Nicassio was choking [her] with two hands. And Ryan [Bush] was standing right behind him. And Larry was choking Trina. Ryan was standing right behind Larry and Justin was standing right behind Ryan. But they were close enough to where all three of 'em could be seen from the kitchen."

Q. "Did you react to this?"

A. "Yes."

Q. "How?"

A. "Well, I jumped up. In the time I was watching, which was maybe two seconds, [Larry] was choking her, I watched him stick his hand in his pocket and pull out a knife. Ryan had a knife also that he pulled out. While I was looking at them, Justin was just watching what was going on with Larry and Trina. Larry was looking at Trina. Ryan was looking at me. And when I was looking at him, he pulled out a knife to show me he had a knife. He pulled it out of his pocket, slid it partially out of his pocket, and slid it right back in just to show me he had a knife. Larry pulled a knife out of his pocket, too."

Q. "What kind of knife?"

A. "Steak knife . . . and Justin was standing there drinking a beer. I jumped up with my beer in hand. From me seeing it to jumping up was maybe two seconds. And I hit Justin in the head with the beer bottle. And then I hit Ryan, and then I hit Larry. Then I hit Larry again, and I think I kicked Ryan in the ribs. And Ryan and Larry stayed on the ground. And Justin and I fought. And he had a large piece of glass sticking out of the top of his head. And he was bleeding a lot. Both of my arms, from my fists to my elbows, were covered in his blood. And he was going at it. He wasn't backing down from me at all. I was giving him foot and backing him back into the kitchen where that stand was with the gopher snake that that guy had got in earlier. And I backed into it, and it started to teeter. I grabbed it with one hand to stop it from falling. Justin grabbed the other side to stop it from falling. We stopped it. It stood up straight. We looked at each other. It was the end of the fight."

Q. "Was it typical where you'd fight with one of the members of your family, one of your brothers?"

A. "Sometimes when you got too drunk, it was done. But it was all understood. It's better to fight with one of your friends than with someone else, 'cause you can go to jail for that."

Q. "Now back to when Larry had Katrina, as you said, choking her. Was Katrina fighting him off?"

A. "Not at all. She had her hands at her side."

Q. "Was she losing color from the [lack] of oxygen?"

A. "Didn't appear to be."

Q. "So it wasn't one of the situations where the person is violently choking somebody?"

A. "She wasn't gagging or anything."

Q. "It looked to you like she was being held against her will?"

A. "Yes."

Q. "And you hit Justin with the bottle?'

A. "Correct."

Q. "But you testified that Justin was the one standing there drinking the beer. You tell me if I'm wrong . . . Justin was the least threat to you or the least threat to Trina. Larry and Ryan were the bigger threats."

A. "They looked like they were all involved in something together. Larry's sixteen years old. Ryan wasn't much older. Justin is older. I've seen Justin fight on several occasions. He knows how to fight. He's good at it. So in the few seconds I had, I had to take out the biggest threat out of it, which was Justin. And the one weapon I had was a bottle, so I hit him first."

Q. "In the Skin Head Dogs, would it be fair to say there's a certain hierarchy?"

A. "Yes."

Q. "Where did Justin fit in, in SHD?"

A. "Near the top. Justin, Mike Wozney, and I."

It was hard to say if Scott Porcho was telling the whole truth or not in this latest version of the events at his party of November 27. But one thing was for sure at the grand jury inquest. Both Ember Merriman and Beverlee Sue Merriman had lied to the grand jury at every point they could about the day after the party and the bloodstains on the stairs. They were trying to distance themselves and Justin as far away from the disappearance of Katrina Montgomery as they could.

Then a very curious thing happened, just by luck, to help Ron Bamieh's cause. On December 9, 1998, Investigator Volpei was going to a meeting with a jail classification unit at the main jail when he happened to notice Justin Merriman's girlfriend, Wendy Applegate, sitting with another woman in the jail waiting room. Investigator Volpei immediately went to the phone to see if Merriman and Nicassio were expecting visitors. When this was confirmed, he held up the meeting while he gathered recording equipment.

Volpei returned to the jail and rigged Nicassio up with a wire. He instructed him to talk about the murder of Montgomery, and say that he was no longer going to be quiet about it since he was taking all the heat, even though he hadn't killed her. Investigator Volpei also told Nicassio that Merriman's sister, Ember, had just testified before the grand jury and told the truth this time, that she'd seen Justin cleaning up blood after the murder. Volpei told Nicassio to confront Merriman with this information and see what happened.

Nicassio went in for the visit wearing a jail shirt rigged with microphones sewn into both shoulders. It had been determined that in earlier recordings the voices were sometimes drowned out by other inmates talking and background noises. Positioning the microphones in the shoulders captured the conversation with the least background noise.

Nicassio first spoke to his visitor, who was not part of the operation and just happened to be scheduled to visit him that day. The fact that Merriman and Nicassio had visitors at the same time was pure coincidence. After Nicassio was through talking to his visitor, Justin Merriman approached him and Nicassio blurted out what Ember Wyman had just told the grand jury. Merriman countered that he had an answer for everything she said, and for Nicassio not to worry about it. They would say the blood was from the cut he suffered in the fight with Scott Porcho.

But Larry Nicassio persisted in trying to trip up Merriman into making a confession, and their exchange became more heated and was caught on tape.

Nicassio: "Hey, you know your fuckin' sister's testifying on that shit, right?"

Merriman: "Yeah. They're tryin' to say some shit about

my mom and now they're tryin' to get my mom in this shit."

Nicassio: "You know, you know that your sister is also testifying."

Merriman: "Everything's good with that. I got blasted on the head." (With the beer bottle). "That's the shit on the fuckin' stairs."

Nicassio: "Oh, oh. Yeah, yeah, yeah."

Merriman: "There ain't nothin' there. But check it out. I don't want nothin' said about my mom. You know what I mean? I'm fuckin' trapped."

Nicassio: "Wait. What?"

Merriman: "Anything said about my mom. There can't be nothin' said. You can't break now. My mom's involved in this. You know what I mean? And if anything's said, [Katrina's body] went over the fuckin' bridge—it never went through the house? Do you hear me?"

Nicassio: "Wait a minute. What?"

Merriman: "If anything is ever said, that shit went over the fuckin' bridge. It never went through the fuckin' stairs and living room. Do you hear me? Because my mom . . . They're saying my mom cleaned up the fuckin' blood."

Nicassio: "Well, but your sister, homes."

Merriman: "There ain't nothin' there. It wasn't her. It was her old man said that she said that."

Nicassio: "But she's saying that she cleaned up the blood on the stairs."

Merriman: "Shut up! That's from that dickhead [Porcho] fuckin' hitting me on the head. There ain't no worries about that. We're going to be fuckin' all right, dog."

Nicassio: "I hope so. But I didn't do this. And I don't wanna do the time for it."

Merriman: "Hey, dog, you can't fuckin' break. You're

talking like this is making me nervous. Why are you sayin' this?"

Nicassio: "Because I don't wanna fuckin' do the time."

Merriman: "I ain't gonna hear you gettin' on like you did that last time."

Nicassio: "Well, you don't fuckin' listen to me."

Merriman: "I'm listening exactly to what you're saying."

Nicassio: "Okay. How do you think I feel? I didn't do this shit, homes."

Merriman: "Hey, man, don't say that anymore."

Nicassio: "What? That I didn't do this shit?"

Merriman: "Hey, I'm gonna tell you one more time. Don't say that to me. I wish you would fuckin' relax . . . Lookit. If you tell me one more fuckin' time that you're innocent, that you didn't have anything to do with it, I'm gonna bust your ass. I'm gonna draw, and that's the bottom line. It ain't gonna look good for either one of us. So don't tell me that. Never again. You hauled [Katrina's body]. I'm just telling you one more time, don't say that again."

Nicassio: [Laughing] "Drama, drama, drama. You know, this whole jailhouse thing really sucks."

One remark made by Merriman really piqued the interest of Ron Bamieh and Mark Volpei. They wondered how Justin Merriman knew that his mother was under investigation and who was tipping him off. This information was supposed to be confidential.

On January 7, 1999, Ron Bamieh had presented enough evidence against Justin Merriman to finally get an indictment from the grand jury for the murder of Katrina Montgomery, resisting arrest, and the rapes of Sally Crocker and Sandra Elmwood. In all it was a twenty-five-count indictment. Merriman, who had been scheduled to face the charges for his standoff on Kellogg Street in court the same week, was in a lot more trouble now. His lawyer in the Kellogg Street incident, James Farley, said he would not handle the murder case because of a conflict of interest.

By now the links of intimidation from Justin Merriman spread out like a vast toxic spill in all directions. Deputy DA Ron Bamieh and Investigator Mark Volpei became determined to find out just how far it went and how deadly it had become. What they could see at that point was only the tip of the iceberg. But they could sense its ominous presence just beneath the surface, and if they weren't careful, it could sink their whole case.

THIRTEEN

A DEADLY GAME OF CAT AND MOUSE

It wasn't long after Justin Merriman was indicted for the murder of Katrina Montgomery that he began conspiring with his mother to contact other members of the Skin Head Dogs in order to plug the leaks of people who were talking to the DA's office. As Ron Bamieh said later, "[Merriman] had previously served a prior prison term and is aware of the prison culture. The defendant is aware that California Department of Corrections inmates will harm and even kill other inmates who have cooperated with law enforcement. The defendant makes it clear to the people he writes within CDC that he wants the information he is providing in his letters, concerning the participation and identities of witnesses, to be distributed throughout the prison system."

On January 26, 1999, a letter was seized by the district attorney's office that had been written by Justin Merriman to a fellow gang member. On the envelope Merriman used the name of another inmate named Patrick McBee on the return address, so that authorities wouldn't think he had sent the letter. McBee had nothing to do with the Montgomery case. Justin addressed the envelope to his mother, and put her name down as Mom McBee. The address was her correct home address. Inside the envelope he placed three letters. (Or piggybacked them, to use a jailhouse term). One letter contained instructions to his mother to send the other two enclosed letters to inmate friends of his who were serving time in other prisons. One letter was going to Brandon Sprout and the other to Brian Smith. Sprout was serving time at Corcoran State Prison and Smith was in the Ventura County Jail. Beverlee Sue Merriman was already on very friendly terms with Brandon Sprout.

Justin wrote her, "I am just waiting for my next visit. Wendy is going to be here, right? I will have another letter going out to you. I got your letter with the newspaper clipping in it."

To Brandon Sprout he wrote, "Look, I really need you out here right now. There is a lot of work to be done and you know how my back is . . . One of the girls who says [I] raped her is that little sawed-off pasty-faced troll, Sally Crocker. She says this happened in '94 or '95. Somebody isn't being charged because they made a deal with the devil DA."

Then he signed the letter, "Peter Goes in Ya."

This confiscated letter really sent up a smoke signal to Ron Bamieh and Investigator Volpei. Merriman was being apprised of information that should have been sealed within court documents. There was no way that he should have known that Sally Crocker was cooperating with the DA's office.

A short time after the letter was seized, Brandon Sprout was interviewed at Corcoran State Prison by Investigator Volpei. Sprout admitted that he had received other mail from Justin Merriman via Beverlee Sue Merriman. He also said after he received it he read the letter, then tore it up and flushed it down the toilet. He wouldn't reveal what the contents were, but he did admit that he was a member of the Skin Head Dogs.

On February 5, 1999, two more letters were seized that emanated from Justin Merriman, pursuant to a search warrant. One was addressed to Stacey Warnock and the return address was Justin, Booking Number 847967. The second letter was addressed to MOMA at Miller Court. Inside of MOMA's letter were other letters that Beverlee Sue Merriman was to send on to various inmates around the state. One was to inmate Harlan Romines and another to inmate Mike Gawlik. Romines was in Wasco State Prison, as was Gawlik. Justin wrote Beverlee Sue in part, "I just came out of the visiting with you and that was quick! It was nice seeing you though. Thanks for coming mom! I wrote a letter for Mike Gawlik. And I got another letter for Harlan Romines. When you put the return address, just write or type 'Peter' and the box return address under it. Don't put my name on the envelope alright? They will know who it is. Thank you for being my mail Mama!"

Then he told her he was going to get back to reading the grand jury transcript. He said he only had two hundred pages of it and that he looked forward to getting more. He finished by saying, "I love you mom and I thank you again for your visit tonight."

To Romines, Justin wrote, "They indicted me a few weeks ago on all kinds of charges. I went from lookin' at sixteen years to the death penalty. Now I received all the paperwork in this. It all starts with Chris Bowen wearing a wire on me while we were cellies in suicide watch when I first came in last year. Maybe you could shoot a letter off to your wife Denise and tell her to page Chris' wife and let her know what kind of man she married . . . a rat man."

Merriman also wrote about Larry Nicassio wearing a

wire on him. Merriman told Romines to inform an inmate named Todd Gladhill about the situation.

In the letter to Mike Gawlik, Merriman stated, "This information I'm fixin' to give you, I want you to pass it along to anyone who will listen in there, especially to the woods from Ventura County. It all starts with this piece of shit Chris Bowen from Pier Point in Ventura wearing a wire on me in the cell when I first came in."

Merriman related that Bowen already had a deal in place with the DA's office and that he might now be at the Wasco Reception Center. Merriman realized that no convict was going to attack Bowen without proof of his helping law enforcement. Merriman wrote, "Look, I know no one's going to bust a grape without seeing paperwork, but the word is already out on this Chris Bowen cause of him telling on Danny [another convict in a different case]."

Merriman went on to describe Larry Nicassio and gave his gang name, "Face." He told about Nicassio wearing a wire in his shirt at the visiting room. Then he described "another bad man" named Mike Bowman who was now in Section 2. Merriman related, "He has 'Peckerwood' tattooed on the side of his neck in handwriting and 11550 on his chest. If you run into a big wood Fuzzy from SFV [Sylmar Family of the Valley] who was in Section 2, run him down on that story, all right?"

In yet another letter, this time to Stacey Warnock, Merriman attempted to get the CDC number for Pee Wee, aka Larry Mason. Merriman told her, "I'd like [Mason] to know what's goin' on. You see his baby's mom [Sally Crocker] is claiming that I raped her back in 1994." Then he said that Chris Bowen wore a wire on him. "And who knows what else he did. He only got three or four years for that bullshit. Spanky, Mike Wozney, was another one I couldn't believe."

Deputy DA Bamieh was stunned by all these revelations.

Justin Merriman was privy to all the inside information of the ongoing covert operations, almost as soon as they were being implemented. There was a terrible leak that had to be stopped. It was putting all the witnesses and informants in the case in grave danger. The only trouble was, at the time Bamieh had no idea where the main leak was coming from.

To help in the matter, Investigator Danny Miller contacted Investigator Wesley Harris, an expert in prison gangs, at Wasco State Prison. Miller's report got right to the heart of the matter. Miller related, "On March 22, 1999, I spoke to Investigator Wesley Harris by phone. Harris said he has been assigned to the Wasco State Prison Gang Unit for approximately the past three years. He has been a correctional officer with the California Department of Corrections for the past eight years. Harris received his gang training from Correctional Officer Ray Rivera, a recognized gang expert.

"For the past three years Harris has developed an expertise [in] prison white supremacist groups incarcerated throughout the California prison system. Several of these groups include the Aryan Brotherhood, Nazi Low Riders (NLR), and Skinheads. Harris wrote the original intelligence report that classified the NLR as a prison gang."

Miller added, "Harris explained when a prisoner arrives at a reception center they quickly learn about the many groups who occupy the prison. The prisoner is indoctrinated to recognize the different prison gangs and treat them with respect that they have earned.

"I asked Harris to explain what would happen to an inmate in the penal institution who was an informant for law enforcement. Harris replied this individual will be targeted to be beaten or killed. All gangs have the same philosophy when it comes to police informants. These individuals are immediately identified to all in the organization and the prison. Harris said informants can expect to be targeted by any prisoner."

When Miller asked Harris about the term "paperwork" that Merriman had used in his letter, Harris said the expression meant written documentation that proved the informant had cooperated with police. He explained that prison gangs require their members to prove another inmate is an informant before they approve a murder or attack that individual. A murder inside the prison interrupted the daily schedule of all inmates, and caused the entire prison to be locked down for an extended period of time. All visits, mess hall privileges, and inmate work schedules would be canceled, which had a very negative effect on the daily business of a gang's drug dealings. To prevent the loss of prison privileges and business, the gang's command structure had to authorize the murder, and the proof they required was commonly referred to as "paperwork," in the form of copies of police reports or court transcripts that included the name of the informant and his statements. As Harris told Miller, "Once the gang's command structure approves the 'hit,' orders are given to eliminate the target."

Deputy District Attorney Ron Bamieh and his investigators now knew they were in a deadly game of cat and mouse with their use of informants to convict Justin Merriman, and his equally deceptive means of eliminating those witnesses. Since so much of the evidence against Merriman was merely circumstantial, the informants were crucial to make their case. And just how far Merriman was willing to go to stop them became apparent as more and more of his letters were intercepted. These letters between him and the others gave not only an insight into his intimidation plot but a glimpse into the Skin Head Dogs' psyches, as well.

Case in point were the letters going back and forth between Justin Merriman and Ian H. Ian H, who was serving time in prison, wrote Merriman when he learned Merriman was incarcerated. "Hey, fag! I got your page o' psycho ramblin's today! Good to hear from you Dog! I miss ya to death brother. I was surprised to open a letter from Jennessa and get a love letter from my favorite J-cat homosexual. Ha, ha."

Ian asked how things were going in Justin's cell and said that he was in C status in a disciplinary building, but would be out of there in a week. He said that things had been pretty wild in his prison with two riots and a couple of fights. With a year to go, he wondered how much more trouble he would get into and dreamed about the days that he and Merriman used to hang out with another gang, the Chiques Vipers. Ian joked that they used to pass off dollar bills for twenties. Then he grew absolutely rhapsodic about the girls he used to know in Ventura.

"Well, it's Valentine's Day again. The one year anniversary of what got me here. Ah, what fun it was. And as for the girls I was fucking out there, I barely remember who they were or their names, stud. I was having a fucking blast out there! That's why Jenny and Jed were calling me foolish, man. I was fucking everything I could get my little white pecker into! Ah, the good times. Oh well, this is the life we chose."

Ian commiserated about Justin's bad luck and complained that in his own reception area they had cut out all smoking. He said it was fucked. "Healthy, but fucked."

Then he complained that the guards had recently confiscated all his property and that they were always hassling skinheads and his "comrades," as he put it.

In Merriman's response, he told Ian how he and another white inmate got into a fight with two black inmates in the holding tank. As he put it, "We beat all the black bark off their asses."

Merriman complained that he was "special housed" in the jail and that it would be at least another year and a half before his trial. He related that his public defender had told him that the prosecutor was seeking the death penalty against him. " They want to give me the last shot of my life, homie! Lethal injection and from what I hear about when they hit you in the main line with that mean shit there ain't no rush to the brain at all. You go to sleep and that's that! No mas Big Daddy Mumroc. No nada!!! Junkie face goes stone dead forever."

Merriman was particularly bitter that his friend Mike Wozney had worn a wire on him, and told Ian that he about went through the roof when he first heard about it. He said he had been running with "Woz" since he was fourteen years old. In Merriman's words, Wozney had made a deal with the "Devil DA" just to get out a few months early. He told Ian how Wozney had tried to trick him into going in a bait car, but that he had overheard someone else on the cell phone and was suspicious. It really bothered him that, of all people, Wozney had done this. They had gotten drunk together and fought together for years. "I've got into so many fights over him being drunk and starting shit," Merriman said. "And then he goes all ass hole backwards on me! I can't stop thinking of it dog."

Merriman kept shaking his head in disbelief that Wozney would do it to get out of jail four months early.

"And this one's gonna blow your mind too," he wrote. "P.wee's first baby's mama [Sally Crocker], that fuckin' silly lookin' flat tire tittied, pasty faced troll, says I raped her yuck butt back in 1994. I can't believe that sawed-off slut."

Merriman also wrote that Sandra Elmwood was saying that he raped her on her father's boat in Ventura Harbor. He called her "a sucked up junky face" and a "stone bone liar."

Then Merriman told Ian to pass the word about Chris

Bowen, who had been in suicide watch with him when he first was arrested. He said he had all the paperwork on him, and that Chris had been looking at sixteen years but would now do only five because of the deal he made with the DA's office.

Merriman also tipped off Ian about Larry Nicassio of the Sylmar Family, who was looking at a "187" (murder charge). He stated that he knew Nicassio had started wearing a wire on him in March 1998. He also knew that Nicassio was looking at a possible eleven-year prison term and that the word should be spread around to get him once he went to a prison. Nicassio was to be fair game for anyone to take out.

According to Merriman, another con to look out for was John C. from the Avenue. He said that John C. was always using meth, and to be on the lookout for him. Then he added, "All I gots to say is there is more wires in this mutha-fucka than AT&T!!! Fuck!!"

He added, "If you are writing Jed, tell him Chris is up there in Ironwood [prison] and let him know what's up with these other fake pieces of shit. Spread the word dirty bird. OK?"

Merriman joked about Ian having to spend 120 days in disciplinary C status. He said, "That will hold ya, you flamin' homosexual!"

While Justin Merriman was on the offensive in one area, the investigators were on the offensive elsewhere. They had finally convinced Ryan Bush to talk about what happened at Scott Porcho's party in November 1992, and the deadly aftermath. Unlike Nicassio, they gave him immunity for everything that he told them. Bush corroborated much of what Larry Nicassio had already said, but he added important new details, as well. He remembered Sylmar Family

skinhead Roman Dobratz spilling beer on the floor at Porcho's party and Justin Merriman rushing up to sock him in
the nose. While Nicassio went to Dobratz's aid, Katrina
Montgomery rushed in, as well. Nicassio pushed Montgomery out of the way. For some reason Nicassio seemed to
be doing everything that Merriman wanted. Bush thought
that Nicassio might have been afraid of Merriman and was
trying to placate him.

At various times during the party Bush heard Merriman
say to Nicassio, "I'm gonna get that broad. I'm gonna get
that bitch!" Whenever Montgomery, who seemed to be
drinking a lot, would come up to try and put her arm around
Merriman, he would push her away.

Much later on, at Merriman's house, while he and Nicassio lay on the floor in sleeping bags, Bush heard a "smack"
sound several times. He rose up and asked Merriman, "Hey,
what do you think you're doing?"

Merriman responded, "What the fuck do you mean?
What does it look like I'm doing?"

What he was doing was raping Katrina Montgomery after
slapping her.

As for the bathroom incident—when Montgomery pleaded
to Merriman that she didn't want to orally copulate him anymore and she needed to go to the bathroom—Bush said he
told Merriman, "Let her go to the bathroom."

Merriman became angry and shot back, "What ya mean,
stupid! She's gonna tell on me."

Another new detail that the investigators didn't know previously was that after Merriman had killed Montgomery
and they were on the way to Sylmar to get rid of her body,
Merriman raided Montgomery's purse for cash and used it
to buy gasoline.

Of all the people who spoke to the investigators about
Justin Merriman, Ryan Bush was the only one that Merri-

man never discovered was "ratting" on him. He believed he had Bush's cooperation and silence to nearly the very end.

Another former Skin Head Dog who was cooperating with Volpei was a man named Jake. He was serving time in a Central Valley prison and afraid that a couple of inmates there were out to kill him for an unrelated incident. He contacted the DA's investigators and said that in exchange for information on Justin Merriman he wanted to be transferred to the Ventura County Jail to serve out his term. Volpei contacted him to see what his story was.

Jake told him that before he was incarcerated he had gone to see Merriman in the county jail. Merriman told him that he had paperwork on Scott Porcho and spelled the word "rat" on the Plexiglass window that separated them.

Jake responded, "A guy doesn't know what to do unless asked."

"Are you serious?" Merriman said.

"Very serious," Jake replied.

Merriman told Jake to come back with a paper and pencil at a later time and he would have instructions for him. "Give me your word that you'll do what I tell you," Merriman said.

Jake gave his word and Merriman told him that he wanted him to kill Scott Porcho. Merriman was especially angry at Scott Porcho and Mike Wozney because they had been his best friends.

Jake never followed through on this request.

On March 4, 1999, Mark Volpei and Ron Bamieh visited Skin Head Dogs members Michael Bridgeford and David Ziesmer at Wasco State Prison. They were there in part because they wanted to see where Bridget Callahan fit into the whole scheme of things. What they discovered was absolutely eye-opening. According to the *VC Reporter,* Ziesmer told them he planned to marry Bridget Callahan when he got out of prison. This news sparked a search of

Ziesmer's cell. What they found were letters from Callahan to him postmarked from Georgia, Texas, Utah, and Arizona. Both Bamieh and Volpei surmised that she was on the run. But on the run from whom? Justin Merriman and his witness intimidation program? Or was it something else?

As for letters found in Bridgeford's cell concerning the Merriman case, Wendy Applegate had written Bridgeford saying, "I miss my J [Justin]. Have you seen the papers? He's big time now. Front page and all."

Soon thereafter, letters were intercepted from Justin Merriman and Stacey Warnock, a Skin Head Dogs girl. Justin had asked her to assist him in spreading around the names of people who had worn wires on him. Warnock's letter of March 17 to Justin read:

> Hey sugar! How's everything going? I just got your letter today. I was beginning to think you had forgotten all about my white ass. Yeah, the last two Saturday nights I went to a meeting in Ventura and saw Wendy [Applegate]. I'm so glad she's getting her shit together. She's cool people. I'm also real happy that she's sticking it out with you. It makes me happy to know that she's there for you.

Stacey went on to write about Sally Crocker and called her a bitch with a big mouth. Just like Merriman, she referred to Crocker as a troll. She said that when Mike Bowman got out of jail, she had gone over to his house but he didn't want to hang out with anyone from the Skin Head Dogs anymore. She thought something was fishy, and now she knew why.

As for Sally Crocker, Warnock said she didn't talk to her anymore. "Fuck a bitch with a big mouth!" she wrote. "I love the little one, though."

Warnock complained that she was on random drug testing and that if she messed up one more time it was probably back to jail for her. At the end of the letter, she gave Merriman addresses for Jim M and Samantha Medina. Medina was serving time in Chowchilla Prison and had a propensity for violence when it came to people she thought were "rats." Stacey was sure that Medina would be helpful to his cause.

Ember Wyman, Justin's long-suffering sister, was not immune to his efforts to draw her into the ever-widening network of conspirators in his cause of witness tampering and intimidation. He wrote her, "I wanna give you a quick run-down on all these wire-wearing pieces of poop. I had [the] dope fiend, Andrea Morrow, coming to visit sometimes and she was doing the same shit, wired." Then he went on to tell Ember about all the others.

Around this time Mark Volpei interviewed Larry Nicassio, and Nicassio showed him a list of five witnesses who had talked to the grand jury about Justin Merriman. Their names were being passed around the jail. The list included John C., Chris Bowen, Mike Wozney, Andrea Morrow, and himself. Nicassio told Volpei that the inmate in the cell next to him had passed him the note, and it had been through other inmates' hands, as well. This inmate told Nicassio that Merriman had said, "Give it to any 'woods' in jail so they can handle it."

Volpei and Bamieh realized they had a very serious problem on their hands. On March 13, 1999, Volpei received a phone call from Andrea Morrow, and she told him about a message her boyfriend had received the previous day. Her boyfriend was a Skin Head Dogs named Spencer, and a friend of Merriman's. The message came from Skin Head Dogs member Ken Barber, who began reading "paperwork" on Andrea Morrow. Barber wanted to know if the guy's "ex-girlfriend" (Morrow) was a rat. Then Barber included some more disturbing news. He said for the boyfriend to meet Beverlee Sue Merriman to get a copy of the paperwork.

With this information, Volpei finally had a good idea who was the main source of all the "paperwork" being passed around. Beverlee Sue Merriman was like the hub of a wheel, connected to all the spokes of Justin Merriman's campaign of threats and intimidation.

FOURTEEN

LINKS IN THE CHAIN

Beverlee Sue Merriman was definitely a vital link in Justin Merriman's web of intimidation. Their relationship, as Ron Bamieh had pointed out, was not the usual mother-son relationship. It went far beyond that. She was not only willing to cover up a crime for his sake, she was now willing to perpetrate new ones on his behalf.

On March 14, 1998, Volpei received another phone call from Andrea Morrow. She was scared and told him that her boyfriend, Spencer, had just received a message from Justin Merriman at the jail. Merriman said that Morrow was a rat and that people had paperwork on her. Merriman went on to say that he would allow Spencer to read the paperwork. When Spencer asked if one of his "people" was Beverlee Sue Merriman, Justin became extremely angry and told Spencer never to bring that name up over a phone line. Then Merriman said that Spencer should not tell Morrow about this phone call, or that he was still collecting paperwork. Spencer ignored his order and told Andrea.

On March 19, Andrea Morrow phoned Volpei once again and said she had just received a disturbing new message on her answering machine. A Skin Head Dogs girl named Samantha Medina had left the message for Spencer, indicating that she needed to arrange a meeting with him. Morrow knew that Medina had a reputation as being a "tough girl" and prone to violence.

Samantha Medina was twenty-six years old. According to court documents, she had dropped out of school in the eleventh grade and never worked except for a few summer jobs during her teens. During her late teen years she was a member of the Ventura Avenue Gangsters. She said she had started smoking marijuana at the age of eleven and began drinking beer at age fifteen. That same year she started snorting crank (methamphetamine), as well, and even tried PCP, an animal tranquilizer.

Medina had some run-ins with the law starting in 1994. That year she was a passenger in a vehicle driven by Justin Merriman's friend, Brandon Sprout. When Sprout's car was pulled over by police for a traffic violation, they found methamphetamine, a gram scale, and a dagger in the car. Sprout jumped out of the vehicle and began running. The officers followed him. As soon as they all took off, Medina jumped in the driver's seat and attempted to escape by driving away. But she was soon pulled over by a squad car and arrested.

In 1995, she "borrowed" a friend's car without permission. The friend did not quite see it that way, and Medina was arrested when she brought the car back.

Then in 1998 Medina was pulled over by Ventura police in a traffic stop. A thirteen-inch knife was found in her possession.

Through her associations on Ventura Avenue, Medina knew and liked Justin Merriman. She admired his tough-guy act. And there was no doubt how she felt about rats. The best thing that could happen to them in her opinion was that they be killed. "I'd go a long way to 'talk' to a rat," she once said.

On March 25, 1999, Volpei spoke with Spencer and asked

him to call Samantha Medina. He did as instructed and left
a message on her answering machine, lying that Andrea
Morrow was no longer his girlfriend. Medina phoned back
and said, "Don't worry about it. I'll take care of the matter
myself when I get back to Ventura."

Because of all the apparent illegal activity emenating
from the Merriman residence, on March 27, 1999, new
search warrants were authorized by the Honorable Bruce
Clark to search the Merrimans' house and property on
Miller Court. During the search, investigators found supposedly sealed transcripts from Justin Merriman's grand
jury proceedings. These were copies identical to transcripts
provided to Justin Merriman's defense attorney by the district attorney's office. Beverlee Sue Merriman was not
supposed to have access to this material, which included information concerning everyone who had worn a wire on
Justin Merriman.

The list of people who were aiding and abetting Justin
Merriman in his campaign of intimidation and threats kept
growing apace. It reached out to Skin Head Dogs member
Jed Malmquist in prison, another man named Robert Imes,
and Skin Head Dogs girl Kara Allen.

The letter to Imes began with Merriman's typical raunchy
humor before he got down to business. "Robbie, I know
your cellie is keeping you pretty busy sucking his dick every
time he comes back from court. You fucking homosexual."

He told Imes to shoot off a letter about the women who
had said he raped them. These allegations of rape really upset
Merriman. In fact, in some ways they made him angrier than
the allegations he had murdered Katrina Montgomery.

Then he told Imes he couldn't wait until Nicassio was out
on a level-four yard. That would be great fun, he boasted.

The other hip prisoners were "going to go in his flat ass all day and one half the night," as he put it.

"Yeah, his ear-biting ass is gonna be with us for awhile. Ten years? He is gonna have to quit making all them deals with those toads. I told him he is even starting to smell like them! He's fucked."

Then Merriman told Imes how he was happy that his girlfriend, Wendy Applegate, was sticking with him. He joked that she was parking on the other side of the building so all the horny inmates like Imes couldn't look at her.

Merriman was getting pretty cocky by the time he wrote P. Funk in another prison. "I just got the third volume of the Grand Jury indictment transcript. There are eleven volumes in all. So there is a lot of shit I haven't read yet but the shit I have read has straight blown my mind brother."

He related about the bait car and Mike Wozney's role in it. He said that it straight "blew my mind" about Wozney. He couldn't believe that he had rolled on him just to get out four months early.

About the report, Merriman added, "It also says Woz called a we-tip hot line from the streets years ago cause he thought I was involved in a [murder] a long time ago. I about went through the roof when I heard about it. I can't stop thinking about Spanky! That fat fuck really hurt me, homie!"

Merriman went on to write about John C., Chris Bowen, and Sally Crocker, once again calling the last a "sawed-off pasty-faced troll."

Then he asked for various phone numbers and addresses, saying that he especially needed addresses of inmates who were serving time in prisons located in the Central Valley. He said he could also use Chrissy's number in "Slimy" (Simi) Valley. He thought she would be willing to help him.

So far, women like Bridget Callahan, Stacey Warnock, Jenny Wepplo, Wendy Applegate, Samantha Medina, and especially his mother had been a big help in Justin's clandestine network.

Merriman went on to say, "The other mud duck who claims I put the pipe to her without her permission is that sucked up needle monster Sandra Elmwood. That blue eyed devil is saying this happened in 1995. I was like, 'Wow!'"

Merriman wrote that he was amazed by the number of people who had worn wires on him and were willing to help the DA's office. He asked when Imes was getting out and to be sure to spread the word on all these people, especially Larry Nicassio. Then he warned him not to put any gang writing in any letters he sent. All letters containing gang writing and symbols were scrutinized right away.

Another part of the intimidation network was Skin Head Dogs member John R. He told Jenny Wepplo, "The only one I know in all the mess is L'il Larry [Nicassio] and he's locked up. So someone's got to get him from in there."

A letter in the network from inmate Jed Malmquist in Ironwood State Prison was particularly graphic. He said, "There is only one thing to do and that is get a mouse trap and catch all these Rodents! I'm not sure if I wrote you about all the madness or not, but Mumrock's [Justin Merriman] paperwork is starting to come in and he was making it *very clear* to me to tell you about cheese eaters in a cell near you. Remember Danny Irish's crime partner that Bridget Callahan had the paperwork on [indecipherable]."

Jenny Wepplo shot off a letter to another inmate that said, "Hey, did you get my letter referring to a fool named Chris Bowen? He's running around Ironwood and Big Daddy

Mumrock says he needs his jaw *wired*. So did you get the [indecipherable] on all that Mumrock paperwork poo poo?"

Just like Beverlee Sue Merriman, Jenny Wepplo was becoming one of Justin Merriman's key distributors of letters and paperwork. She wrote Malmquist, "Tell all the brothers on that yard when cheeseboy is to get that deal making wire wearing punk out of—well, he's just an oxygen wasting fool! And those bitches [Crocker and Elmwood] will go down in flames, burning!"

In a letter back to her, Jed Malmquist wrote, "Chris B [Bowen] is being transferred somewhere up north. He's just waiting on a bus, there really ain't no shit that can be done. He's on a different yard and I have no paperwork on him. I sent word, but . . . I guess he'll be out in about two more years. I still haven't heard from Bridget. What's up with that? Has anyone out there seen her? Weird!"

As for the absence of Bridget Callahan, Jenny Wepplo wrote back, "About Bridget??? Things that make you go, ummm, ummm! *No one* has heard from her . . . at all! I've heard some way out shit and I can make up some weird shit in my head as well."

Among the Skin Head Dogs there was reason to be concerned about the disappearance of Bridget Callahan. She knew a lot, not only about the murder of Katrina Montgomery and the disappearance of Nicole Hendrix, but about the ring of witness tampering, as well. No one knew if she was talking to the investigators, on the run, or if something more sinister had happened to her. If Montgomery and Hendrix could disappear for good, it could happen to Bridget Callahan, as well.

Justin Merriman might have been less jocular and cocky in his letters if he'd known that Deputy DA Ron Bamieh and

Investigator Mark Volpei were now close to shutting down his main means of distributing letters and paperwork, none other than Beverlee Sue Merriman. Even then, he must have caught a whiff of what was about to go down, because he sent off a letter to Jenny Wepplo saying, "Hey, sistah, that hoe you mentioned in your mail [Morrow] was coming to visit with a wire on my mom and working best she could with the devil DA. You know I would like to call and tell her old man, Fat Boy, what time it is . . . You see I did time with her old man in the joint and he would cut that hoe loose in a heartbeat. All those pieces of poo-poo in my paperwork are all making deals to get out of shit and they are making me as the bad guy."

Wepplo's reply to an old acquaintance on this score was:

Hiel! The shit over here is way out!!! You might already know by now that P. Wee, Bridgeford, Ian, Sal, your brother and also Loodee and that fool Spyder— and myself—we all received Grand Jury subpoenas to testify to prove there is enough evidence to indict Justin on Intimidation of witnesses and if so then we'll get indicted on accomplice or just witness intimidation, and so *any* mail that talks about Justin and *cheese*—please dispose of them ASAP—for everyone's safety or they'll end up as evidence.

She complained that the DA's office had been issuing search warrants and seizing her mail. She warned not to piggyback letters since all these were being read. Wepplo said that a man named Jerry was "trippin' " because of all the stuff the DA's office knew about Merriman's intimidation network. Then she begged that no one else write her at her PO box. "It's all for our safety!" she exclaimed.

She said that someone named Jerry was on his last days

of freedom and since her grand jury appearance she didn't know how long her own freedom would last. She wrote that the shit was going down pretty hard in Ventura County and that anywhere except there was starting to look good. She added that he needed to keep his head up and they would do fine.

She signed off and managed to work a swastika into the "y" at the end of her name.

Jenny Wepplo didn't have long to wait and see just how "shitty" things were going to get in Ventura County. On June 16, 1999, she was indicted for conspiracy to intimidate and threaten witnesses. She was the latest person that Justin Merriman had brought down in order to save his own neck.

Meanwhile, Samantha Medina was also contacted by Investigator Volpei for her threats to harm Andrea Morrow. Medina admitted to being part of Justin Merriman's network of intimdiators and she was very up-front about it. She told Volpei that she believed "rats" ought to be hurt or killed. She said she had gone to Andrea Morrow's place of employment in Ventura to talk to her and make her shut up. But Morrow had not been there that day. Medina said that she would have beat her up if necessary. She did not indicate if she would have killed her.

On the same day as Jenny Wepplo, Samantha Medina was indicted for conspiracy to intimidate a witness by force or threat of force. The indictment read in part:

> While in custody Justin Merriman has contacted many people, including Samantha Medina, other inmates, his mother and a number of friends to dissuade victims and witnesses in these pending matters from

testifying against him. Since some of these witnesses are themselves in custody in the state prison system, he has attempted with the help of his friends to get the word out that they are 'rats' which would cause them to be attacked and/or killed in prison. In the cases where the witnesses are themselves victims he has tried to conspire with others to intimidate them from testifying.

In the current matter, Andrea Morrow has testified as a rape victim against Merriman and has worn a wire to record the defendant's statements. She is currently pregnant with Spencer's child and they have a relationship together. Spencer has a history of affiliation with skinhead gangs and has been in prison four or five times.

On March 25, 1999, Samantha Medina spoke to Spencer on the telephone. She told him his girlfriend was a 'rat,' knowing the consequences for that label could mean Morrow might be hurt or killed. She also inferred that she would take care of the matter herself when she got back into town.

Samantha Medina came from Madera to Ventura and went to Morrow's former place of employment looking for her. Medina has a mental health history and has been known to carry a knife. On one occasion she displayed her knife to Spencer and Morrow.

At the actual grand jury inquest, Samantha Medina was less than contrite. She bragged about how "all rats should die." It was such blatant gangsterism that Ron Bamieh said later, "The grand jury wanted to indict her right after she took the stand. She admitted with a great deal of pride what she did. As a prosecutor, it was one of the most chilling pieces of testimony I've heard in a while."

Samantha Medina probably regretted her bold statements later. She pleaded guilty to the charges on July 20, 1999. At her sentencing phase she said she had learned the error of her ways. She said that she had gone to Morrow's place of work knowing that she wasn't there at the time, only with the intention of scaring her. "I took my two children along with me. I knew she wasn't there. I wasn't gonna start any trouble, especially in a public area . . . It's usually my mouth that gets me into trouble. I'm sorry for the trouble I caused."

Superior Court Judge Art Gutierrez gave her a full year in state prison to think about the trouble she caused. Ron Bamieh commented, "The court made it clear he was disgusted by [Medina's] actions."

So far Justin Merriman's web of intimidation had brought one person after another down with him. And by midsummer of 1999 Ron Bamieh and his investigators had the biggest target of all within their sights—Justin's mother, Beverlee Sue Merriman.

FIFTEEN

HAND SIGNALS

Things were heating up for everyone by the summer of 1999. On June 14, Larry Nicassio was sentenced by Superior Court Judge Edward Brodie, after being found guilty for conspiracy in the death of Katrina Montgomery. Nicassio's lawyer, Darren Kavinoky, warned the judge that if Nicassio served any prison time he would be set up as a target to be killed. Kavinoky said, "Because of his cooperation, there is now a contract out for his life. I think Mr. Nicassio has suffered more than any of us know. He has carried this around for years." Kavinoky pleaded with the judge to keep Nicassio in the county jail or placed under house arrest.

Even Ron Bamieh was sympathetic to a degree with Nicassio's plight. After all, Nicassio had played a big part in helping him and his investigators crack the case. Bamieh said, "Quite frankly, when [Nicassio] first told us where her body was buried, and the circumstances, we didn't believe him." But as time went on, Mark Volpei's investigations corroborated what Nicassio was saying. Bamieh went on to relate, "[Nicassio] has done everything we've asked. He has risked his life. Frankly, we have put him in situations where if he were found out, he could have been killed."

In the end, however, Judge Brodie was not going to let

Larry Nicassio off without some prison time. He said, "It is unconsciable what happened in this case. I've seen a lot of carnage and death in my day. This goes beyond belief."

Judge Brodie sentenced Larry Nicassio to three years in state prison. Exactly two days later, on June 16, Beverlee Sue Merriman was indicted for conspiracy to intimidate witnesses.

Evidence against Beverlee Sue Merriman as the hub of the conspiracy had been mounting all spring and reached a crescendo by June 1999. During the search of her home there was a discovery of supposedly sealed court documents not open to the public, listing all of the witnesses who had worn wires on Justin Merriman, and various letters from gang inmates.

One confiscated letter in particular was about to trip up Beverlee Sue Merriman. She wrote to an inmate named Sal Sponza at Tehachipi State Prison, "I talked with Justin and he is finally in good spirits. His emotions are running up and down with the documentations that he's been reading with what [the wired individuals] are saying about him."

She shouldn't have known anything about documents concerning wired individuals that were supposedly sealed under court order.

Then Beverlee Sue added, "I want you to know if anything were to happen, I will be there for you also."

The "smoking gun" that proved that Beverlee Sue Merriman knew the illegality of her activities came in late June. Sergeant Cox at Tehachipi State Prison sent the DA's investigators a tape-recorded phone conversation between Beverlee Sue Merriman and Sal Sponza's cellmate, Johnny Wayne Drake. During the conversation Beverlee Sue said, "If you have anything in your cell that is not copacetic, get rid of it." After this statement she could no longer claim that she didn't know what kind of illegal activity was transpiring in the letters she was "piggybacking" to other inmates on Justin's behalf.

Beverlee Sue Merriman was indicted of conspiracy along with Justin Merriman in June 1999. The indictment read in part that they had conspired "to intimidate witnesses by force or threat of force." It was further alleged that the conspiracy was committed to promote Justin Merriman's gang, the Skin Head Dogs. She was also indicted of another conspiracy to induce false testimony before the grand jury as to Justin Merriman's rape and murder indictments.

The indictment against her included twenty-nine illegal overt acts. It started by saying, "The 1998–1999 Ventura County Grand Jury hereby accuses Beverly [*sic*] Sue Merriman of committing the crime of Conspiracy to Commit a Crime in violation of section 182 (a) (1) of the Penal Code, a felony. She did willfully and unlawfully conspire together and with another person, to wit, Justin Merriman, to commit the crime of Inducing False Testimony in violation of section 137 (c) of the Penal Code."

The various overt acts were a veritable laundry list of threats against all the witnesses who had spoken out against her son or helped in the investigation. They ran the gamut from Overt Act 1, "Assistance in intimidating and disuading witnesses upon Mr. Sprout's release from prison," to Overt Act 29, "Beverlee Sue Merriman speaks to Jake M., a known member of the Skin Head Dogs criminal street gang, in order to arrange for police reports and for Grand Jury transcripts about Justin Merriman's case to be given to Jake M."

There was a special allegation at the end of the indictment. It read, "It is further alleged pursuant of the Penal Code 186 22 (b) (1) that the above offense was committed for the benefit of, at the direction of, and in association with criminal street gang, to wit, the Skin Head Dogs, with the specific intent to promote further and assist in criminal conduct of gang members." By roundabout means, Beverlee Sue Merriman had finally become a Skin Head Dogs girl.

She was to be held on $120,000 bail. Judge Donald Coleman restricted her mail and phone calls to her son. But interestingly enough, he did not restrict her visitations, judging that they could be monitored.

Justin Merriman was indicted with a similar list of threats and intimidation against witnesses, especially Larry Nicassio, John C., Christopher Bowen, Andrea Morrow, Mike Wozney, and Scott Porcho.

To put an end to all the "paperwork" being illegally delivered to Justin Merriman, the judge in the case laid down strict guidelines as to what material and what visitors Merriman could receive in jail while he awaited trial for rape and murder:

Good Cause Having Been Shown, the court Hereby Orders: The defendant Justin James Merriman shall not violate any provision of Penal Code section 136.1. The defendant is not to contact, either directly or indirectly, by any means whatsover, any witness who testified before the Grand Jury in the case of *The People of the State of California v. Justin Merriman*. The defendant is not to have any contact by any means with any gang member or gang associate; including, but not limited to, the Skin Head Dogs. The Ventura County Sheriff's Department is to prohibit the defendant from using the telephone while incarcerated in the Ventura County Jail. The Ventura County Sheriff's Department is ordered to review every incoming and outgoing letter, or piece of mail the department believes is directed to or from Mr. Merriman. Any incoming piece of mail from inmates within the Department of Corrections or discussing any witness involved in this case will be turned over to the court and reviewed for release to the District Attorney's Office and representatives of Mr. Merriman.

All visits with the defendant, except between Mr. Merriman and his attorney and/or investigators and/or experts, will be monitored by the Ventura County Sheriff's Department. The Ventura County Sheriff's Department is to house Mr. Merriman in whatever part of their custodial facility to facilitate compliance with these orders. Willard Wiksell [Justin's lawyer] and/or his investigator are prohibited from providing Mr. Merriman material not originally created by Mr. Wiksell's office or retained expert, except discovery which must be examined pursuant to Paragraph 9 of this order. Specifically, Mr. Wiksell's office is prohibited from acting as a messenger for Mr. Merriman by providing him with communications from individuals in an attempt to circumvent the Court's order that all of Mr. Merriman's incoming and outgoing mail be reviewed by the Sheriff's Department.

Justin Merriman and his attorneys and investigators are ordered not to provide any materials made available to them via the discovery process to any other individuals. Mr. Wiksell and Mr. Maxwell and/or their investigators may review discovery material with witnesses, but that material must stay within the dominion of Mr. Wiksell or Mr. Maxwell and/or their investigators.

It is so ordered.

Incredibly, even with an indictment upon her and strict orders against tampering with the judicial process, Beverlee Sue Merriman continued to try and circumvent the court order and the DA's office, just to help her son. But by now Mark Volpei was on to all her tricks, as well as those of Justin Merriman. Beverlee Sue continued to visit Merriman in the jail visitors' room, unaware that Volpei was video-taping and audiotaping their conversations.

He commented later that audio and video recording devices were placed in one of the visiting rooms within the Ventura County Main Jail for the purpose of monitoring Mr. Merriman's visits. Volpei explained that he'd been present on August 10, 17, 24, 31, and September 7, 1999, when Beverlee Sue Merriman visited Justin at the Ventura County Main Jail. Each visit had lasted approximately one hour and every visit was recorded. Later, Volpei reviewed the tapes, watching them over and over. As he did he began to notice that Beverlee Sue and Justin Merriman used hand signs and verbal signals to communicate with each other. Because Volpei was already so knowledgeable about Justin's case, he was eventually able to interpret some of their verbal and nonverbal signals. He noted that Beverlee Sue Merriman frequently spelled witnesses' names on the glass that separated visitors from inmates.

One signal that Justin and Beverlee Sue often used was their thumb and fingers coming together to describe witnesses who had cooperated with the district attorney's office. They also mimed physical appearances of witnesses, such as a beard or tattoos. They even made a gesture like a pen writing to symbolize certain letters. It became clear to Volpei that Justin and Beverlee Sue believed they were being audiotaped, but that they didn't know that they were being videotaped as well.

On August 10, 1999, Beverlee Sue Merriman visited her son and surreptitiously discussed several witnesses. Justin described his displeasure about his sister's testimony at the grand jury hearing, and then he discussed two of his rape victims. Beverlee Sue stated she would try contacting one of these victims.

On August 17, 1999, Beverlee Sue met with Justin on another visit at the jail. During the visit Justin asked if she had hidden certain evidence so that it could not be obtained by the district attorney's office. Beverlee Sue indicated that the material was safe at a friend's house. Based on what Volpei already knew about these two, he deduced that they were hiding some incriminating letters at a friend's house.

On August 31, 1999, at another meeting, Justin spelled out the names of two men that he wanted to be intimidated by other gang members. He told his mother that they were "bad men" and not to be trusted.

In a meeting on September 7, 1999, Justin pantomimed the beard that John C. wore, and told Beverlee Sue that he needed to be watched. He also wrote out the name of a rape victim on the glass and said that she had to be dealt with. Finally he praised his girlfriend, Wendy Applegate.

Beverlee Sue replied, "She's really doing good right now."

"I know, and tell her so," Justin responded.

Then he wrote the letter "L" on the glass, which stood for Larry Nicassio, and said that he needed to be taken care of.

He also wrote the letters that stood for Ryan Bush. Justin still considered Bush one of his allies, not knowing that by now Bush was helping the prosecution in their case against Merriman.

Justin briefly brought up the name of Kermit Lucas, who was also in the jail at that time. Investigator Volpei already knew that Merriman's mother, Wendy Applegate, and a girl named Lisa had put money on Lucas's sbooks at the jail. Volpei also learned that Beverlee Sue had tried disguising her name when she signed the property slip by writing the initials SQ. These initials stood for Suzie Q, one of Beverlee Sue's nicknames. Lucas later told Volpei that in exchange for the money, Justin wanted him to send out his letters hidden within Lucas's outgoing mail. Lucas told Volpei that he had refused.

In summation of all this illegal activity going on between Justin Merriman and Beverlee Sue Merriman, Investigator Volpei wrote the court, "Beverlee Sue Merriman continues to be a serious danger to the witnesses in the case against Justin Merriman and in the case against her. I have reasonable cause to believe that Beverlee Sue Merriman's current bail status is insufficient to assure the protection of the victims of her offense. For reasons stated above, I request that bail be raised in Beverlee Sue Merriman's case to two million dollars."

Meanwhile during this period, Samantha Medina was being sentenced for her part in the conspiracy to intimidate witnesses. Judge Art Gutierrez gave her a year in county jail and three years' probation. He said, "I would have sent you to prison if not for the fact you admitted to the crime."

Ron Bamieh chimed in about his displeasure with Medina. Then he noted about other gang members that there were seven others still under investigation for witness tampering. "Some have indicated a desire to work with us; however, some have run for safety. Those who have decided to run, we're not going to chase now. But at the end of Mr. Merriman's trial, we will find them." High on his list of those who had run was Bridget Callahan. Both Bamieh and Volpei believed that Callahan might have some key evidence to help them. Now all they had to do was find her. If she was still alive.

When it came to the assessment of how Beverlee Sue Merriman fit into this complex web of deceit, Bamieh wrote the court:

> [She] attempted to cover up her son's murder when she committed perjury in front of the Ventura County Grand Jury. The defendant continued in her attempts to cover up her son's murder in her subsequent illegal agreements with her son to dissuade Mr. Nicassio from cooperating with the police, and then to help Mr. Merriman intimidate and dissuade witnesses.
>
> The defendant was motivated to participate in these crimes due to her obsessive relationship with Mr. Merriman. The defendant has consistently tried to please Mr. Merriman throughout her adult relationship with him by performing any task he demands. Mr. Merriman controls the defendant. The defendant obeys Mr. Merriman and her role in this relationship is to do what he asks without question.

And yet, despite the increase in bail, despite all the punishments facing her, Beverlee Sue Merriman was willing to do even more for her son. She was ready to face serious jail time in his cause by committing another flagrant act of disobedience to the court order, and bring one more person down with her.

SIXTEEN

WITH FRIENDS LIKE THESE

A new wrinkle to surface in the Beverlee Sue Merriman/ Justin Merriman conspiracy to dissuade and intimidate witnesses had its origin back on August 23, 1999. On that date Beverlee Sue was being arraigned and Tamara Green, a friend of hers and a lawyer, announced to the judge that she would represent Beverlee Sue Merriman in her case of conspiracy and witness intimidation. Judge Brodie asked Ms. Green if she was representing Beverlee Sue for all purposes, including the trial, and Tamara Green said that she was and requested a January court date.

Investigator Volpei was already aware that Willard Wiksell and Phillip Capritto were representing Justin Merriman. Tamara Green at this point was not Justin's lawyer. Wiksell and Capritto did have an investigator, Fred De Fazio, helping them, but there were no other lawyers helping on their case. Due to the very restrictive court measures of September 17, 1999, absolutely no one else was to have court records or documents concerning Justin Merriman's case. In fact, Justin Merriman was to have no other visitors except Wiksell, Capritto, and De Fazio. He could not have visitors or receive letters or phone calls without the court's monitoring and approval.

Supposedly privy to this knowledge was Tamara Green. She had been served a copy of the People's Motion to Increase Bail on Beverlee Sue Merriman on September 27, 1999. Within the motion was a phrase that noted the only people allowed to visit Justin Merriman were Wiksell, Capritto, and De Fazio. To be fair, this information was buried near the back of the document and easily missed.

Nonetheless, on January 29, 2000, at the Venutra County Main Jail, Sheriff's Record Technician Connie Rous looked up from her desk and was surprised to find Tamara Green standing there. Ms. Green identified herself as a lawyer and asked to visit Justin Merriman. Green completed a jail visiting form and Connie Rous ran a routine computer check to determine Justin Merriman's current housing location. During this check, Ms. Rous discovered that Justin Merriman was not to have any visitors other than Wiksell, Capritto, and De Fazio. There was a note attached to contact the Inmate Classification Unit for further information. Rous telephoned Inmate Classification and spoke to Deputy Bornet, who suggested a noncontact visit. This meant that Tamara Green and Justin Merriman would have to be in separate rooms as they spoke to each other via the telephones.

Tamara Green refused this arrangement, since the rooms contained video and recording equipment. She cited lawyer/client privilege. When Ms. Rous questioned her about the problem with the setup, Tamara Green said she'd personally seen videotapes of visits in those two rooms. Unsure of what else to do, Ms. Rous placed Tamara Green and Justin Merriman in Room 1, a full-contact room where they discussed matters that went unrecorded. This meeting went on for a lengthy amount of time, and later Tamara Green would state that she thought they were together for about three hours. What they discussed would become a matter of grave concern.

Somehow, Sergeant Bonnie Gatling found out about the meeting that was taking place and knew that Tamara Green was not on the list of people allowed to see Justin Merriman. She immediately contacted the watch commander, Sergeant Jeff Allaire.

Sergeant Allaire went to the room where the meeting was taking place and asked Ms. Green to step out of the room and into a secured hallway. He told her he wasn't questioning whether she was an attorney, but he did need to know why she was visiting Justin Merriman. As Green started to speak, he interrupted her and told her to be very careful with her answers. He said he wasn't threatening her, but the situation did not seem right and they were going into a very tricky legal area.

In his report Sergeant Allaire later wrote, "Ms. Green stated that she was representing Justin Merriman's mother in her court case. Ms. Green said she was familiar with Justin's case and has been involved since June of last year. Ms. Green said Justin's mother's trial would be over sometime in February and she was considering being involved in Justin's representation after that. Ms. Green stated that she was in contact with Mr. Willard Wiksell's Office and they suggested an interview with Justin Merriman. Ms. Green wanted to talk with Mr. Merriman to see if she wanted to be involved in his case."

Later Sergeant Allaire would tell Investigator Volpei that during this episode Tamara Green "looked nervous." She only mentioned that she was there to see Justin Merriman about possibly being his representative later. According to Allaire, Green did not mention anything about checking on his health status or that of Beverlee Sue Merriman, something that Tamara Green would claim later. This business about health concerns would become a very important point.

None of this might have become known to Investigator

Mark Volpei except for a chance encounter. On February 4, 2000, Volpei telephoned Ember Wyman about a letter that was recently mailed to her. During the conversation, Ember told him that she was worried about her mother's health and that Beverlee Sue wasn't receiving proper medical attention. In response, Volpei said he would check into it.

On February 7, 2000, he learned that Beverlee Sue had been transferred to the medical facility at the main jail and he went there to check about her condition. When he arrived at the medical housing unit, he asked if Ms. Merriman was receiving proper treatment. He said that someone was worried about her and had asked him to check on it. Beverlee Sue replied that she was not, but that she was taking care of it. Volpei spoke to the nurse, who said that Beverlee Sue's condition was stable and that she would soon be returned to the honor farm.

On February 8, Volpei received a telephone call from Tamara Green. She asked why he had been to see her client without her being present. Volpei told her the reasons, but she thought it was still wrong that he had done so. Then she revealed some startling information. She said that she had been to visit Justin Merriman at the jail. As she put it, "I received a call from Mr. Wiksell, who said [to] go there and see him. I would have preferred to go with him."

Volpei knew that no one was supposed to be visiting Justin Merriman at the jail except Wiksell, Capritto, and De Fazio. He told Ms. Green this and she responded by saying that she was not aware of the court order barring everyone except those three from visiting Justin Merriman. She then gave Volpei an outline of what she and Justin Merriman had discussed. She said she'd given him a full admonition prior to talking with him, and held up her hand for him to stop talking if he discussed his own case. She said, "I didn't hurry, I was there quite a bit."

After her visit with Justin, Tamara Green said she had gone to see Beverlee Sue Merriman at the honor farm. Then, according to Volpei, she told him the only reason she'd gone to see Justin Merriman was to check on his health. But according to Sergeant Allaire, Green had not mentioned this fact once.

All of this rang alarm bells with Volpei. He and Ron Bamieh had just gone through a year of conspiracy between Justin Merriman and Beverlee Sue Merriman in their quest to make the intimidation of witnesses cease. Were these two now trying to use Beverlee Sue's own lawyer as a go-between in their illegal dealings? Bamieh and Volpei intended to find out.

After his talk with Tamara Green, Volpei phoned the honor farm and discovered that Green had visited Beverlee Sue Merriman for approximately an hour after she had spent time with Justin. This made matters look even worse. On February 15, 2000, Volpei went with Bamieh to a meeting with Willard Wiksell and Fred De Fazio. Mr. Wiksell said he had never spoken with Tamara Green about visiting Justin Merriman. He also said that Tamara Green was not associating with him or going to help him defend Justin Merriman. However, he did say that he had spoken with Fred De Fazio about Green visiting Justin Merriman.

De Fazio told them that he called Ms. Green on either January 27 or 28, 2000, and told her that Justin Merriman wanted to speak with her regarding Beverlee Sue Merriman's case. De Fazio also said that she had asked him to accompany her to visit Justin Merriman, but because of other obligations, he couldn't.

On February 15, 2000, Ron Bamieh and Mark Volpei went to Courtroom 12 for an appearance on the Beverlee Sue Merriman case. When Tamara Green approached, Bamieh told her he was troubled by her visit with Justin

Merriman and that he was going to file a motion with the court about her actions. In response, Green said she had never been served a copy of the order banning everyone except Wiksell, Capritto, and De Fazio from visiting Justin. Bamieh in turn told her that a copy of the order was attached to the motion for a bail increase in Beverlee Sue's case. She replied that she hadn't read that part of the motion.

Bamieh said that he had spoken with Willard Wiksell and that his statements contradicted hers. Green responded that she had spoken with Fred De Fazio on the matter and thought everything was all right.

But Bamieh lowered the boom. He said he was in the process of writing a motion and would file it with the court under seal. He said the motion would be filed under her name and it probably would not be picked up by the press. Tamara Green asked, "Should I be concerned about this issue?"

Bamieh replied, "It shouldn't be taken lightly. It could effect your ability to practice law."

Ron Bamieh had gone out of his way to prevent the press from getting wind of this latest flap in the Justin Merriman case, and cause embarrassment for Tamara Green. But Green caught him by surprise. It was she who went to the media instead of hiding from them. She sat in on an interview at a Ventura radio station, KVTA, on February 16, 2000.

The newscaster began by saying, "The attorney for the mother of a Ventura murder defendant is in hot water for visiting her client's son in jail. Tamara Green represents Beverlee Sue Merriman on charges that she was part of a conspiracy to intimidate witnesses against Justin Merriman."

The newscaster went on to tell of Merriman being accused by authorities of being a skinhead racist, rapist, and murderer. He related that Green said her troubles began when she went to see Justin Merriman in jail over a civil matter that had nothing to do with his murder case.

The newscaster mentioned that Green told Justin Merriman that she could not represent him in the civil matter, and that ended the discussion.

Green replied, "I wasn't speaking to him about Beverlee Sue, and very specifically we did not speak of the case and had no intentions of speaking of the case."

The newscaster then related how Green was facing fines or maybe even worse.

Green said, "I found it shocking and I find it very, very difficult to proceed in the face of that kind of power in the defense of a common citizen of this county, who is the mother of a son that she believes is innocent. An exact quote from him, 'It could affect my ability to practice law.' "

Soon after this broadcast, Investigator Mark Volpei filed a report: "Based on my knowledge of the investigation . . . Ms. Green appears to have willfully violated the lawful order of September 20, 1999, issued by the Honorable Judge Vincent O'Neill."

Deputy DA Ron Bamieh's report on the matter was even more direct and accusatory.

At first glance, Ms. Green's visitation of her client's son at the Ventura County [Main] Jail may appear relatively harmless. However, to those who know how dangerous and manipulative Mr. Merriman and his mom are, Ms. Green's contemptuous actions are startling.

Mr. Merriman and his mother pose a significant risk to the public safety of the citizens of Ventura County. Both Mr. Merriman and his mother have been indicted for conspiring with each other to intimidate witnesses by force or threat of force.

Beverlee Sue Merriman's bail is set at $2,000,000.00.

Her bail was raised from $120,000.00 because of public safety concerns. Judge Brodie raised her bail after he viewed a videotape which caught Ms. Merriman and her son surreptitiously communicating with each other in the jail visiting room about certain witnesses involved in his case.

Now, Ms. Green, the attorney for Ms. Merriman, goes to the Ventura County Jail and visits her client's coconspirator when the court has ordered no one other than his attorneys and/or investigators may visit him. This unauthorized visit lasted more than three hours. Later that same day Ms. Green went and visited her client at the Honor Farm for an hour. I have an ethical duty as an officer of the court to report a potential violation of the court's order. And this is what I have done.

Tamara Green argued back:

I met with Mr. Merriman to discuss a potential malpractice lawsuit against the county for various health problems he suffered while in jail. We did not talk about his case. I had worked on a medical malpractice case for another inmate who died last year after being refused proper treatment. The notion that I would run out and tamper with witnesses or that I am a coconspirator is an absolute insult. The brief filed by the Deputy District Attorney Ron Bamieh is a ploy to prevent me from preparing for Beverlee Sue Merriman's conspiracy trial. It has pulled my focus away from that case. It's a matter of an attorney fighting for her life the week before she has to fight for the life of her client."

As to why she had gone to speak with Justin Merriman in the first place, she said that Willard Wiksell had approached her about the health of his client and said that, "He wasn't getting proper medical care." Would she look into it?

Her response was, "I was surprised. I said, 'Sure. Why not? When can we all go? And they said, 'You can go on your own. You're an attorney.' At that very moment I became in my mind an agent of [Merriman's] lawyer. Every criminal defendant in jail has a right to speak with a lawyer. I take serious personal issue with the idea that I fall into the category of a visitor."

With Tamara Green's ability to practice law on the line, Judge Vincent O'Neill weighed all the evidence and ruled that her actions caused him concern but his order had been for general visitors and not specifically about Tamara Green. Then he went on to clarify exactly what his original order meant so that nothing like this would happen again. Tamara Green had survived a close call. She told the press, "It was very hard fought. Judge O'Neill was very concerned about this issue. But this clears my name."

Ron Bamieh made the best of the ruling by saying, "We understand the court's ruling. We are happy that we could clarify the order now so we can avoid any further problems."

Justin Merriman had the unusual knack of dragging just about everyone he knew into the Montgomery murder quagmire. And by March 2000 his sister, Ember, and his mother, Beverlee Sue, were right in the middle of it. On March 22 a very reluctant Ember Wyman sat on the stand testifying for the prosecution about her mother in the Beverlee Sue Merriman conspiracy trial. She had been given immunity for her own perjurious statements to a grand jury. She told about the fateful morning of November 28, 1992. Often tearful and angry, she explained to the jurors how she had lied during grand jury investigations about helping to clean the blood off the stairs along with her mother.

"Why did you lie?" Ron Bamieh asked her.

"I was scared," she responded. "I didn't want people to think something horrible like that happened at my house. I was afraid my family would be in trouble."

Further evidence of Beverlee Sue Merriman's cleanup attempts that day were given by Jeremy Rice, who had been Ember's boyfriend at the time. He told the jury that he arrived to find a very distraught Ember. He related, "Ember was nervous and scared. She said she'd spent all night [*sic*] helping her mother clean bloody footprints off the stairs. She thought something terrible had happened. Then she said that Justin told her, 'I'm going to hell for sure for what I've done.'"

Even Wendy Applegate, Justin Merriman's now ex-girlfriend, was less than helpful to Beverlee Sue Merriman while on the stand. Wendy said, "[Beverlee Sue] said she could have perjured herself." And in another reference Wendy said, "She used to give us money for drugs."

Larry Nicassio was there, as well, implicating Beverlee Sue Merriman in the elaborate witness tampering scheme. He told the court, "I was waiting in [Katrina Montgomery's] truck while Justin and Ryan brought her body down the stairs wrapped in a pink blanket. They climbed in the cab. They were both excited and upset. I heard Ryan say to Justin, 'I can't believe your mom saw us.'"

One of Beverlee Sue's defense attorneys, Richard Hanawalt, objected that this remark was hearsay. But Judge James Cloninger allowed it, saying that it was a spontaneous statement permissible by law.

Nicassio went on to discuss at least two occasions while he and Justin were in the court's holding tank where Beverlee Sue Merriman set up a four-way meeting so that they could get together to construct a witness tampering scheme.

Tamara Green countered that these meetings had been orchestrated by the prosecution to entrap Mrs. Merriman in activities that she didn't know were illegal.

About the only witnesses not giving testimony against Beverlee Sue Merriman were Brandon Sprout and Harlan Romines. According to *Los Angeles Times* reporter Tracy Wilson:

> After shuffling into court with chains around his beefy frame, Romines spelled his name for the court clerk, then stiffened his back and shut his mouth.
>
> "I refuse to answer any questions," he repeated.
>
> "Did you tell [the witness, an informant in the Justin Merriman case] that he wouldn't be safe in any prison yard?" Deputy District Attorney Ron Bamieh asked.
>
> Romines would not answer that question and three others posed by Bamieh. As a result he was held on four counts of contempt for willfully refusing to answer questions. He was fined $4,000 and ordered to serve twenty days in jail—not that the sentence had much effect.
>
> "I'm already doing a bunch of time, so what does it matter?" Romines chuckled from the witness stand. Then he said, "If I answer any questions, my life ain't worth a penny. I won't jeopardize myself for any case."

Eventually it was Beverlee Sue Merriman's turn to take the witness stand in her own defense. But something very curious happened as Ron Bamieh tried to introduce an audiotape of one of the wired conversations between Larry Nicassio and Justin Merriman while they were in the county jail. While Bamieh argued to have the tape introduced as evidence, Beverlee Sue Merriman read over the transcript of that tape. She reached the portion where Justin told Nicassio, "That shit [Montgomery's body] went over the bridge." Suddenly, without warning, Beverlee Sue began crying hysterically. Before long she was absolutely wailing.

Ron Bamieh was thunderstruck. He admitted later, "I guess that was the first time she looked at the transcript. She broke down and started crying to the point we had to cancel the proceeding for the day. Mrs. Merriman asked to be excused to the sally port area. She was yelling out, 'I can't believe he did it! He did it!'"

Beverlee Sue had something to cry about. On the audiotape Justin Merriman had all but admitted to the murder of Katrina Montgomery. Not even she could look the other way now. She had witnessed something being carried in a blanket over that footbridge on the morning of November 28, 1992. Now she knew for certain what was inside that blanket.

Beverlee Sue's defense lawyer, Richard Hanawalt, said, "She became virtually uncontrollable. She kept saying, 'I didn't believe it. I didn't believe it.' This lady had genuinely been in denial."

The next day in court Beverlee Sue Merriman changed her plea from not guilty to guilty in the charges of witness tampering. Through a stream of tears she turned directly towards Katy Montgomery, Katrina's mother, and said, "I'm sorry, I'm so sorry. I didn't know."

When Justin Merriman read in the newspaper about his mother's sudden breakdown in court, he could hardly believe it. He wrote her, "Mom, you should see the big L.A. *Times* of Ventura County section article of 4-29. I don't really know what's with you or why you wigged out in the courtroom. But those tricks. Bamieh and Hanawalt sure talk a whole lot of dukey. [Hanawalt], is he working for the District Attorney's Office or is he wanting to get his name in the paper? What's his trip?"

Justin quoted Hanawalt as saying, "She was awakening to

the fact her son must have actually done it. She became virtually uncontrollable. She kept saying, "I didn't believe it.'"

Justin asked her, "Is this another DA trick?"

Justin said he had read the article fifty times and still hoped it was fiction. Then he drew an angry face on the letter. "It's got to be [fiction]," he said. "Damn those newspaper staff writers. Lying to be lying, and making mountains out of molehills."

It took three more months before Beverlee Sue Merriman faced sentencing. Ron Bamieh argued before Judge Cloninger, "Your Honor ought to make an example out of her. I say put her in prison. That's where she belongs. Send a message that Ventura County will not tolerate witness intimidation."

On the other side, Richard Hanawalt said that Beverlee Sue Merriman had become an unwitting accomplice when Justin asked her to piggyback letters to other prisoners. "This is something the prosecution doesn't understand," he said. "Mothers do tend to love their sons."

But in the end, Judge Cloninger wasn't buying that argument and he told the court, "I have before me a person who thinks she has done nothing wrong. She is out of touch with reality."

Judge Cloninger sentenced Beverlee Sue Merriman to two years in state prison for her crimes. Beverlee Sue Merriman blinked once, then buried her face in her hands.

SEVENTEEN

"LIKE DÉJÀ VU
ALL OVER AGAIN"

Investigations were leading in several directions for Deputy DA Ron Bamieh and Investigator Mark Volpei during the fall of 1999. There was one person who knew all about the murder of Katrina Montgomery and disappearance of Nicole Hendrix—Bridget Callahan—and she had been missing for months. But in October of that year, Volpei was finally able to track her down. Callahan was by now living in Phoenix, Arizona, and working in a veterinary office as a receptionist.

Bridget Callahan was such an important figure in the Merriman case that both Bamieh and Volpei took a trip to Arizona to talk with her. At this point, Callahan was just a witness and not a suspect in anything, except for possible witness tampering. When they showed up, she seemed almost relieved to see them, according to Volpei. He sensed that she was tired of being on the run. Callahan told them she'd turned over a new leaf and said that she would talk about Justin Merriman and the murder of Katrina Montgomery.

Volpei phoned Ventura County Sheriff's Detective Cheryl Wade and told her that he'd found Callahan. Wade, who was working on the Nicole Hendrix case, wanted to talk to Callahan in person about Hendrix's disappearance. But Callahan only wanted to speak with Bamieh and Volpei, whom she trusted at this point.

The next morning, what was supposed to be only a short meeting turned into a marathon. The questioning first focused on Justin Merriman and Katrina Montgomery, and Callahan was very forthcoming about facts related to that case. She stated that Justin Merriman had told her he killed Montgomery, and that he had also used her in his witness intimidation scheme. But somewhere along the line, Callahan veered off into the disappearance of Nicole Hendrix. There things began to get very sticky for everyone involved. The Hendrix case was still officially a Ventura County Sheriff's Department case and not the province of either Ron Bamieh or his investigator, who were both with the district attorney's office. But as Ron Bamieh explained later to the *VC Reporter,* "We met Callahan at the restaurant and spoke to her for about two hours. Just about the entire conversation was spent talking about Merriman. During our conversation Callahan asked me about [Larry] Nicassio and I told her that he was in a room and saw something terrible happen. Callahan replied, 'I can relate.'"

According to the article, Volpei told her that Detective Wade from the sheriff's department was in town and wanted to talk to her [about Nicole Hendrix]. Callahan told him that she would rather talk to Mark and him. In response he said that they knew nothing about that case and that she should talk to the sheriff's department.

Things became even murkier. Although Callahan had been very up-front in talking about Merriman and Montgomery, she was reluctant to talk to the sheriff's department about Nicole Hendrix. It took Mark Volpei several weeks to convince her she should go back to Ventura County and speak with Sheriff's Detectives Cheryl Wade and Bill Gentry about the case. Finally, Callahan said that if she did talk to them, she wanted protection. Mark Volpei told her he thought that might be possible.

On December 22, 1999, Bridget Callahan returned to Ventura, but instead of going to see the sheriff's detectives as planned, she dropped in at Mark Volpei's office, unannounced. In a moment of absolute candor she blurted out everything that had happened during the murder of Nicole Hendrix and her own part in it.

Volpei immediately phoned Detective Gentry, who paged Ron Bamieh. Even with the cat out of the bag, Callahan still insisted on speaking to the sheriff's detectives only in the presence of Bamieh and Volpei. Ron Bamieh contacted one of his superiors in the DA's office and received permission to be present. But the waters were indeed murky by now and would come back to haunt everyone concerned.

Bridget Callahan told Bamieh, Volpei, Wade, and Gentry that she would explain everything about the murder of Nicole Hendrix only if she received full immunity, received protection, and was relocated to New Mexico. Ron Bamieh said he would bring this up with his superiors.

Bamieh then spoke with Ronald Jones at the DA's office and told him their predicament. At this point in time, Bridget Callahan was their only witness in the murder of Nicole Hendrix. Bamieh wrote up a simple outline of an offer to Callahan, saying she would receive $3,000 in moving expenses and protection. In return she had to tell them everything she knew about the murder of Nicole Hendrix.

Jones didn't like the deal and said it was too lenient. He had Bamieh add one very important proviso. This deal would only stand if Bridget Callahan was in no way a participant in the murder of Nicole Hendrix. The word "participant" would become a very grave matter of semantics.

Bamieh in turn was not happy with this new development. He argued that they needed her just as much as she needed them, since there were no other witnesses. Without her testimony, the whole case might fall apart like a house of cards. But Jones stuck to his guns and the amendment stayed in place.

Ron Bamieh wasn't happy, but he took the agreement back to the sheriff's office and explained the details to Callahan. He said later that he made it a point that if she was a "participant" in the crime, all deals were off and she could face criminal proceedings herself. The others present remembered him saying this, as well. The exact quote was, "In the process of providing a statement you either are untruthful or have intentionally misrepresented your involvement, then we cannot reach an agreement with you. Any statement you have made to law enforcement will be used against you and you may be subject to prosecution."

Bamieh asked if she understood. Callahan said that she did. But exactly what she understood became a matter of significant conjecture. Callahan seems to have thought that she was no more culpable for the death of Nicole Hendrix than Larry Nicassio had been in the murder of Katrina Montgomery. And Nicassio had received a fairly good deal from the district attorney's office. Perhaps acting on some misguided beliefs, she signed her name to the document and sealed her fate.

Bridget Callahan told those present that she had witnessed the murder of Nicole Hendrix at the City Center Motel in Ventura, instigated by David Ziesmer and Michael Bridgeford. But with mounting horror, both Bamieh and Volpei realized that she had helped keep Hendrix there for the others to kill and had acted as a guard while they did it and later got rid of her body. In her own mind, she may have thought of herself as being no more culpable than Larry

Nicassio at the Katrina Montgomery murder because he had been a witness and then helped get rid of the body. But Callahan's actions had been far more serious than Nicassio's. In some ways, she had ensnared all of them in a trap from which they would have an extremely tough time extracting themselves.

Things became a morass for Callahan, Bamieh, and Volpei from this point on. They had all gone into the meeting acting in good faith, but semantics and the law had them tied up in knots. The amendment on which Jones had insisted bound Ron Bamieh's hands. Because of the proviso, he could not give Bridget Callahn immunity. She was more than just a witness, she was a participant.

The next morning, Bamieh reported to Jones about the predicament. They both agreed that they had used her ignorance as a tool against her. Bamieh wrote later, "We decided to use her ignorance to get Ziesmer and Bridgeford . . . [She] asked several times what was going to happen to her on the case. I told her the same thing every time, 'Everybody would be held responsible for what they did.' "

Apparently Bridget Callahan did not understand just who *everybody* included. She kept on telling more and more details that tied her directly to the murder.

Acting on a tip, Ventura County Sheriff's Department investigators found Nicole Hendrix's skull, jawbone, and some teeth amidst bits of broken cement up in the mountains. And while they were doing this, Bridget Callahan began wearing a wire, like many others had done before her in the Merriman case. Except she was doing it on Bridgeford and Ziesmer for the murder of Nicole Hendrix. It's ironic that Callahan was helping the very people who would destroy her.

By August 2000, there was enough evidence gathered against Bridgeford and Ziesmer to swear out an indictment against them for the murder of Nicole Hendrix. Unfortunately for Bridget Callahan, the grand jury brought in an indictment against her, as well. This did not set well with Ron Bamieh or Mark Volpei. Callahan had been cooperative with them about this particular crime, as well as in the Merriman case. In Bamieh's estimation, Callahan's charges should have been dropped to voluntary manslaughter, the same deal Larry Nicassio had received. But their superiors did not see things that way.

Ron Bamieh wrote to these superiors, "True, we made no promises in this case, but in our agreement with her it is stated that she will only work as an informant if we believe her and we also do not consider [Callahan] a suspect. When we work someone and give them that the impression that we are on her side, we need to take that into consideration when deciding what are the appropriate charges."

On August 14, 2000, Bridget Callahan spoke before the grand jury about the murder. Bamieh was so concerned for her vulnerability there that he wanted to address the grand jury himself and tell them that she had never been promised immunity in December 1999, and since then she had been taken advantage of by the DA's office and sheriff's department. Everything that had happened was legal, but the ethics were very questionable. According to one source, he wanted to tell the grand jury that if they thought Callahan's charges were too harsh, they could reduce them. (Court records do not reveal if he was in fact able to tell them this, since all grand jury testimony is sealed).

Whether he talked to them or not, on August 17, 2000, the grand jury indicted David Ziesmer, Michael Bridgeford, and Bridget Callahan of first-degree murder in the murder of Nicole Hendrix, with the possibility of the death penalty being imposed.

Among the others charged in the case were James Bowman, with two counts of accessory to murder and two counts of perjury, as well as being the member of a violent street gang. Roy Ashlock was charged with being an accessory to a felony, conspiracy, and committing crimes for the benefit of a street gang. And Kellie Rangel, a girlfriend of Ziesmer, was indicted for committing perjury to help the Skin Head Dogs.

While Nicole Hendrix's mother sat silent in court and didn't speak to the press, David Ziesmer's mother was more talkative. She told *Los Angeles Times* reporter Tracy Wilson that her son couldn't have stabbed Hendrix to death. She said that he was a racist, but he had spent most of the last twelve years in prison because of an unfair justice system. "He was not a violent person," she said. "David is a racist, I'm sorry to say it, but he is. But he has never beat anybody up. I think he is just taking the blame for other people. I know he didn't do it."

Of course, Ron Bamieh had a very different take about David Ziesmer. He told the press, "It was a very gruesome murder. The method in which she was killed was vicious, and the way they treated her after she was dead was also shocking. I know from the cases I've worked, they are extremely violent. We now believe [the Skin Head Dogs members] are responsible for two extremely violent murders of two innocent young women."

A few days later David Ziesmer told a *Ventura County Star* reporter in a jailhouse interview, "I kinda screwed myself. I stepped up and took the fall for everybody, which I shouldn't have done. Everybody involved in this was pointing the finger at me." However, Ziesmer wouldn't tell the reporter if he had stabbed Hendrix to death, but he did say he witnessed it.

Then in September 2000, to paraphrase Yogi Berra, "It was like déjà vu all over again." From his jail cell David Ziesmer began to emulate Justin Merriman in the intimidation and threatening of witnesses. Deputy DA Ron Bamieh and his investigators found letters of a conspiratorial nature going back and forth between Ziesmer and others. Bamieh sought and received a court order to monitor Ziesmer's mail and visitors. As Bamieh told reporters later, "[Ziesmer] has made it clear he wants to kill someone. He's taken steps for them to be killed. So far he's named four people." In his private moments Ron Bamieh must have wondered where any of this was going to stop.

Letters seized from Ziesmer and wired individuals revealed just how far he was willing to go. In one letter he wrote, "[They need to die] because they all jumped the gun and ratted. As soon as I get sentenced all kinds of whacking will be going on."

In another letter he stated that he wanted James Bowman, Brett Davis, and Bridget Callahan killed by a Pleasant Valley State prisoner named Donald Scoggins. Scoggins nickname was Nazi, and Ziesmer wrote, "I love Nazi and feel his loyalties are to be trusted. We're telling him to hit a grand slam instead of a home run." (Grand slam referring to the bases being loaded with Bowman, Davis, and Callahan, who should all die.)

Besides Bridget Callahan, Michael Bridgeford had also decided to come on board with the DA's office and wear a wire on Ziesmer. While they were placed in the same cell, the recording device picked up a conversation from Ziesmer, who did not know that Bridgeford was now working against him. Ziesmer said, "I want the [witnesses] to disappear while I'm in prison. I'm the voice of the Skinheads."

It wasn't long, however, before Ziesmer was on to Michael Bridgeford's wire act and he threatened to have Bridgeford's girlfriend and grandmother "taken care of."

But Ziesmer targeted his most virulent hatred toward Bridget Callahan. It wasn't enough that the state threatened her with the death penalty. Ziesmer wanted it to happen much sooner than that. He actually contracted with another inmate who was getting out soon to have Callahan killed. Little did Ziesmer know that the inmate in question was an informant wearing a wire on him for the district attorney's office.

On September 6, 2000, a court order had to be put into effect on David Ziesmer, just as one had been put in place regarding Justin Merriman, forbidding all mail and visitors. The only people who could now visit Ziesmer were his lawyer and his defense investigator.

In November 2000, Deputy DA Ron Bamieh was ready to make some deals on the Nicole Hendrix case. Roy Ashlock, who drove the pickup with her body in it, pleaded guilty and agreed to testify against the others. Since he hadn't been directly involved in the murder, he received no prison time.

Even James Bowman pleaded guilty and was given a break for testifying against the others.

Christmas was not a merry season that year for David Zeismer. His lawyer, Richard Loftus, asked Judge Art Gutierrez to allow Ziesmer to receive a visit from his mother. Loftus said, "How about some sympathy for his mother? The visit should be allowed in the interest of humanity."

But Deputy DA Ron Bamieh, with thoughts of Beverlee Sue Merriman's transgressions in mind, said, "There's another mother in this courtroom who is not going to see her daughter for Christmas because Mr. Ziesmer killed her. The defendant has done nothing to deserve a visit. We should not be in the business of cutting this man a break. He cannot be trusted, and by inference, people who visit him cannot be trusted."

Judge Guttierez agreed and said, "From a moral standpoint, [Loftus has] an argument . . . but [Ziesmer's] a danger to the community."

David Ziesmer received no Christmas visitors.

Another person not in the holiday mood was James Bowman. On December 20, 2000, Judge Bruce Clark sentenced him to three years and four months in jail, and to pay Nicole Hendrix's mother $25,000 in restitution.

Shelly Holland, Nicole's mother, was at the sentencing of James Bowman, and her testimony was dramatic, to say the least. She held up a small vial attached to a necklace. Inside the vial were Nicole Hendrix's ashes. "This is what's left of my daughter!" she cried. "After Nicole disappeared I feared that her body might be found dropped by the side of the road. My worst fears came true."

Nicole Hendrix's aunt, Konnie Caid, growled from the stand, "[Bowman] would have treated roadkill with more respect."

The murder of Nicole Hendrix and its judicial proceedings were as much a quagmire as the one concerning Katrina Montgomery had ever been. Just about everyone connected with it became tainted, as if they'd been spattered with mud. Michael Bridgeford was running as fast as he could from his skinhead association. Eventually he had his lawyer, Steven Powell, try to obtain an agreement so that he could remove the neo-Nazi and skinhead tattoos from his face. Powell argued, "The continuous view of the defendant with the hideous insignia on his face is going to unduly influence the jury."

But prosecuting Deputy District Attorney Patricia Murphy shot back that the tattoos were evidence. "It has absolutely everything to do with the killing," she said.

Judge Vincent O'Neill agreed with Murphy and denied the removal of Bridgeford's tattoos.

Bridget Callahan was also trying desperately to extricate herself from the net in which she had enmeshed herself. She took on a lawyer, Joseph O'Neill, who had the same last name as the presiding judge. Her lawyer pulled out all the stops in his efforts to claim that his client had been used as a pawn by the district attorney's office. Joseph O'Neill said, "The inducements and promises made to this defendant by the prosecution team were intended to coerce and improperly induce Ms. Callahan's testimony. [They] created an evil scheme to compel her cooperation. The immunity agreements were created in such a way as to confuse Ms. Callahan and take advantage of her."

Even Ron Bamieh had to agree with Joseph O'Neill up to a point. In his presentation to the grand jury he had stated, "We knew as investigators and as a prosecutor that she, in fact, was not a witness. Under the law she was culpable. Miss Callahan agreed to wear a wire. We never let her know at that point that she was culpable. We decided to use her to get Mr. Bridgeford and Ziesmer."

In memos within the district attorney's office, Bamieh wrote, "We took great advantage of her ignorance. We did not lie to her, but we did create the impression that Callahan was helping herself the entire time we were using her."

Defense attorney Joseph O'Neill went way beyond Bamieh's outrage at the circumstances. He became absolutely poetic in his statements to the court. In one motion he wrote about Ron Bamieh and the DA's office, "This sordid pact with the Devil clearly indicates that the desire to convict at any price has swapped hard-won integrity and professional respect for personal benefit and political reward. [It's] a scandalous tale, a Faustian bargain for favorable publicity, made at the price of ethics, morality and a soul that quickly disappeared on a rapid path to Hades."

To which Ron Bamieh replied about Joseph O'Neill, "He's a nut."

One of the few people who did not find the squabbling between Joseph O'Neill and Ron Bamieh amusing was Nichole Hendrix's mother, Shelly Holland. She was too busy living through her hell. According to a story written by Tracy Wilson of the *Los Angeles Times*, "During the past few months, Holland, 40, of Ventura has appeared five times as a guest speaker for the Student Truancy Offender Program, which strives to keep youths cited for truancy in class and out of Juvenile Hall. Though it is difficult, she talks of her experiences because she knows firsthand that skipping school and doing drugs often lead to more serious crime, and she hopes that her daughter's story will prompt some teens to rethink the choices they make."

The article told how Mrs. Holland scanned the faces of the truants who were slouched in chairs and barely paying attention to her. She passed around a faded photograph of her daughter and a tiny silver and glass vial that she wore on a chain around her neck.

"'So what do you think this is?' she asks teens as they silently examine the finger-thin decanter. 'No guesses? This is my daughter in this little bottle. She called one night and said, 'Mom, I'll be right home, leave the door open.' And when I got her back, all that was left was three ribs, her head, and her pelvic bone. That is why she fits in the little bottle.' "

As the year 2001 began, Bridget Callahan's long judicial nightmare was just beginning. But for Justin Merriman the end of a long trail toward justice was finally coming to an end.

III

DAY OF RECKONING

EIGHTEEN

SHOUTS IN THE COURTROOM

In January 2001, while the Nicole Hendrix case progressed in fits and starts, the one for Katrina Montgomery was finally coming to a conclusion. Nearly nine years after Justin Merriman raped and murdered Katrina Montgomery, his day of reckoning was at hand. Inside a packed courtroom, before Superior Court Judge Vincent O'Neill, Jr., Merriman sat beside his defense attorney, Willard Wiksell.

Deputy DA Ron Bamieh came charging out of the gate in his opening statements about Merriman. He told the jury, "On January 30, 1998, those police officers weren't chasing a man riding his bike without a headlight or a man with a gun. Those police officers were chasing evil. He was a desperate man who tried anything to avoid prosecution. This trial is going to be about the defendant running," he said, looking directly at Merriman.

In his daylong presentation, Bamieh conducted a multimedia show with photos projected upon an overhead screen and audiotapes of Merriman's voice. In the audiotapes, jurors could hear Merriman mumbling to informants who had worn wires. It became very clear why his gang name was "Mumbles." Bamieh also presented letters that Justin had written to Katrina Montgomery while in prison.

The day's proceedings were not without unforseen drama. While Judge O'Neill read the charges against Merriman, an alternate juror suddenly panicked and exited the courtroom without a word to anyone. Judge O'Neill proclaimed a twenty-minute recess while the juror was brought back in without any explanation to the press. But all the journalists present surmised that the juror had been frightened by Merriman's ties to the Skin Head Dogs and the campaign of witness intimidation.

The next day, Merriman's defense attorney, Willard Wiksell, had a very different take on the case than Bamieh. He began by praising the way Ron Bamieh had presented his side of the story. But then he said, "What [Bamieh's] performance lacked was evidence that Justin Merriman killed Katrina Montgomery, raped anyone, or tried to intimidate witnesses. What it was, was a theory, because no evidence has been brought forward. The investigators never found Montgomery's body, don't have a murder weapon, and never got Merriman to confess. There is not one piece of evidence that connects Mr. Merriman to this homicide."

Wiksell then raised the question of who would gain the most if Justin Merriman was found guilty of murder. He said it would have to be Ryan Bush and especially Larry Nicassio. It was Nicassio, Wiksell said, who had been standing behind Katrina Montgomery at Scott Porcho's party, pretending to plunge a knife into her head. Nicassio even made the famous sounds from the movie *Psycho* as he did it. It was he and Bush who had buried her body. And now, according to Wiksell, they were trying to place the blame on Merriman.

"[The prosecution] would create a get-out-of-jail-free card on the back of Mr. Merriman," he said. "Larry Nicassio didn't come forward for six years until his lawyer got him a deal. [Investigators] used inmates wearing concealed electronic devices to try and get Mr. Merriman to talk about what happened, but you're not going to hear anything that amounts to a confession. No body, no murder weapon, no confession."

Deputy DA Ron Bamieh's first witness—a very tearful Katy Montgomery, Katrina's mother—certainly kept the jurors spellbound. She told the story her daughter had related to her about Justin Merriman's attack when Katrina had gone to his house to tell him to stop phoning and harrassing her. This tale did differ somewhat from an earlier version told by Shawna Burgess-Torres, Katrina's friend. Katy Montgomery said, "It was late and Beverlee Sue Merriman asked [Katrina] if she wanted to stay over. As [Katrina] lay in a bed in a guest room, Justin crept into bed with her and rubbed himself against her. He was pressing himself against her and making sexual advances. He said, 'You know you want it.' Katrina escaped by saying she needed to use the bathroom and ran from the house."

Then two women who had been raped by Justin Merriman took the stand, as well. Sally Crocker often cried as she told of her humiliation and pain at Merriman's hands. She said, "I was scared and humiliated. How was anyone going to believe me?" Of the incident where she had been tackled and raped in his bedroom, she recounted, "He forced me to have sex with him for hours until I bled on his bedsheets. When I told him it hurt he said, 'Quit whining and shut up!'"

On cross-examination Willard Wiksell asked her why she hadn't come forward to the police earlier. Crocker answered, "I was scared of him and his friends."

All the questioning was going pretty well for Ron Bamieh until Scott Porcho got on the stand. Porcho was wearing a blue Ventura County Jail jumpsuit since he was incarcerated for assault with a deadly weapon. Bamieh asked Porcho to tell what had occurred at the party on November 27, 1992. The questioning went according to plan until Porcho said that Nicassio, not Merriman, had held a knife to Katrina's throat, pinned her up against a wall, and he was the real threat.

Stunned by this reversal of stories, Bamieh said, "You're telling us now that Mr. Nicassio took a knife and put it to Miss Montgomery's throat?"

"Yes," Porcho responded.

As Bamieh asked him more questions along this line, he kept receiving answers that contradicted what Porcho had told the grand jury earlier. In absolute frustration Bamieh said, "What you're trying to do, Mr. Porcho, is protect the defendant."

"I have no reasonable purpose to do that," Porcho replied. "I'm trying to do the right thing and I don't know if I'm frustrating you or what."

He certainly was frustrating Ron Bamieh. Everything he said now put the onus on Larry Nicassio and Ryan Bush. Things became very contentious and Bamieh said, "You never told police what [Nicassio] did with a knife that night."

"I've said that many times before," Porcho replied.

"To law enforcement?"

"Ever since I decided to tell the truth," Porcho said.

In fact, Scott Porcho had told so many different versions of the "truth" by now that it was hard to keep up with them.

On cross-examination, Willard Wiksell offered two police reports where Scott Porcho had indeed told law enforcement agents about the knife incident. He then asked Porcho, "Are you shading your testimony now for any reason at all?"

"I'm trying to be honest as possible here," Porcho replied. "And I think I'm doing a pretty good job."

Things were even more ominous in court the next day. While an informant who had helped the DA's office was on the stand, two friends of Justin Merriman sat in the courtroom. As the informant responded to questions, the two men stared at him and slowly shook their heads from side to side. One of them loudly whispered, "Mumrock," one of Merriman's gang nicknames.

Justin turned around and acknowledged his two supporters.

This brought an instantaneous response from Judge O'Neill. He had the attorneys and bailiff approach. After a short talk, Judge O'Neill cleared the courtroom and had the two men escorted into another room. After twenty minutes they were told to leave the courthouse and not return.

By January 18, things were back on track for Deputy DA Bamieh. On that day, Andrea Morrow told of the prolonged attack on her while she was forced to service Merriman in his room while he looked at porno magazines. She told the jurors, "I didn't say anything [at the time]. I just stayed there. I didn't know what to do."

She also spoke about the incident with the syringe full of blood.

"He told me, 'Shut up or I'll cut your throat like Trina.'"

Larry Nicassio, Bamieh's star witness, took the stand on January 19, 2001. As he spoke of the rape and murder of Katrina Montgomery, tears ran down the faces of the Montgomery family. And through most of his testimony, Nicassio was just as tearful.

"After Justin stabbed her," he said, "she yelled, fell over, and said, 'Please, Justin, don't hurt me!'"

"What did he do next?" Bamieh asked.

"Clubbed her in the head with a wrench and slit her throat."

Later Nicassio spoke of telling a friend about the murder.

"I was afraid and ashamed of what happened. For not doing anything about it."

"Do you feel responsible?" Bamieh asked.

"Yes," Nicassio replied. "For not doing anything to stop it."

Willard Wiksell, on the other hand, wasn't buying any of Larry Nicassio's "innocent bystander" routine. He said that Nicassio's actions at Scott Porcho's party were just a preliminary to what he really did later to Montgomery. Especially the scene he pantomimed from the movie *Psycho*.

"That whole thing was just a joke," Nicassio countered.

"It was you with the knife?" Wiksell asked. "You had the knife three times pointed at her."

Nicassio admitted he did have a knife out, but he did so on the instructions of Justin Merriman.

As for why Nicassio would want to kill Montgomery, Wiksell proclaimed that she had spurned Nicassio's affections at the party and it made him very angry.

Nicassio did admit that he had been attracted to Katrina, but that he didn't kill her.

Wiksell asked, "So in the bedroom [during the actual murder] you've got two cousins in the room doing what?"

"Standing on the side, looking out the window," Nicassio cried. "It was the most horrific thing I ever saw."

"You cried in front of the grand jury, cried while testifying Friday in superior court, and cried during an interview with me. Why didn't you cry the night she died? I will submit you didn't cry because you killed her, Mr. Nicassio. Did you kill her?"

"No, I did not," he responded.

Later, Wiksell spoke of the deal Nicassio made with the district attorney's office. He accused Nicassio of holding out on information until he was arrested in 1997. "You were thinking 'deal' the moment you got popped, weren't you?"

"What I was saying then was I wanted to get what I deserved," Nicassio replied.

Ryan Bush was just as tearful on the stand as his cousin Larry had been. He corroborated much of what Nicassio had said and added a few more details. Bush said, "I remember hearing a whack, and I looked up and Katrina was holding her throat. She was begging for her life. Merriman hit her with the wrench and then tried to hand it to me."

"Why didn't you try to stop it?" Ron Bamieh asked.

"Because I was a coward," Bush admitted.

Wiksell questioned Ryan Bush about the grave he had dug for Montgomery and how large it was. Bush responded, "It was about five feet deep and five feet long. I don't know how long it took me to dig it."

"So, the only persons who know where the body is buried is you and your cousin," Wiksell said. "And if you and your cousin are lying and she's buried twenty miles from there, nobody would know, right?"

"Objection!" Ron Bamieh exclaimed.

"Sustained," Judge O'Neill said.

By the end of January 2001, Ron Bamieh's monthlong parade of witnesses was through. In contrast, Willard Wiksell only had two. And one of them was a handful for him as well as for Bamieh. She was Beverlee Sue Merriman.

Beverlee Sue took the stand wearing a new hairdo, and smiled at her son, sitting at the defense table. She had just recently been released from prison after having spent five months there for her part in witness tampering and intimidation. About the early morning hours of November 28, 1992, she testified that she'd heard her son come home with some male friends and go to his room. She told the jurors, "I guess like any mother I was relieved that he was home."

Then she offered some new information never heard before. "I heard what sounded like pouring water. I looked outside my bedroom window and saw the back of a bald man urinating off the bridge that goes to Justin's room." She said that a recent meeting with the defense's investigator, Art Hernandez, had sparked this memory.

Wiskell asked, "Did you hear any loud noises coming from Justin's room?"

"I heard nothing that night," she responded. "When I woke up at seven A.M. I noticed small drops of blood on the stairs and cleaned them up. About thirty minutes later I saw Justin near his room and asked him, 'Who got hurt?' He showed me a cut on his head and I told him he needed stitches. He said, 'Don't baby me.'

"I stayed at the house until one-thirty P.M. and never saw Justin leave."

Asked about the time that LAPD officers came to her house, she replied, "I let them in. They looked around Justin's room and left. I didn't want my son getting into any trouble."

This revelation totally contradicted Officer Hiem's report on the incident. He had written that she never let any of them into the house and told him to get a search warrant.

After her testimony that day, Beverlee Sue Merriman quietly mouthed twice to Justin, "I love you."

The next day it was Bamieh's turn to question her, and the sparks began to fly almost immediately. He began with a conference between himself, Willard Wiksell, and Judge O'Neill about Beverlee Sue Merriman's complete turnaround about her own guilt in the witness intimidation scheme. Between her trial and the present she had changed her story. She now contended that she'd put on a crying act and pleaded guilty on the advice of her lawyers. Bamieh wanted to show that nothing she now said could be trusted.

Bamieh said, "It's apparent she had a complete change of

heart in between trial and her probation officer and here at this trial. And the People's position is that it's based on [Justin]. I think it's probative in not only their relationship but in her demeanour and testimony. The jury knows that she pled guilty. They know she went to prison. They know she's obviously biased in favor of her son by her answers here in minimizing his involvement with the gang and calling them a 'boys club.' It's relevant to her credibility. She has none and should not be taken seriously."

Bamieh then turned directly toward Beverlee Sue Merriman and asked, "Isn't it true you told your probation officer [about the outburst in her own trial], 'I started crying and crying about everything that was going on. Justin told Larry for him to say "that shit [Montgomery's body] went over the bridge." And that was the first time I was aware that Katrina Montgomery could have been in my home'?"

Beverlee Sue: "I may have said that comment. I don't remember. Everything was like a roller-coaster ride."

Ron Bamieh: "Well, let's get off the roller coaster one second, Mrs. Merriman. The fact is at your trial you apologized. You said, 'I'm sorry. I'm sorry,' directly to the Montgomery family. Is that true?"

Beverlee Sue: "My attorney told me to say those things."

Ron Bamieh: [Incredulous] "Your attorney told you to say those things?"

Beverlee Sue: "Yes, that's the truth."

Ron Bamieh: "She said to turn towards me and Investigator Volpei and act distraught as you could?"

Beverlee Sue: "Yes."

Ron Bamieh: "Cry as hard as you could?"

Beverlee Sue: "Yes."

Ron Bamieh: "And then look over at the victim's family and say, 'I'm sorry. I'm sorry'?"

At this point, Ron Bamieh was nearly shouting at Beverlee Sue Merriman, and Willard Wiksell jumped in. He asked the judge, "Your Honor, maybe we could have him turn down the volume a bit."

Bamieh decided to move on to another area that he found completely outrageous. It was her new story about the bald-headed boy urinating off the footbridge that led to Justin Merriman's room.

Ron Bamieh: "When you heard that boy, that skinhead, urinating off the bridge—"

Beverlee Sue: [Interrupting] "He was going to the bathroom off the top of the bridge into the flower bed."

Ron Bamieh: "Oh, he hit the flower bed?"

Beverlee Sue: "I assumed he did."

Ron Bamieh: "That's because you saw him do that?"

Beverlee Sue: "No. I heard it."

Ron Bamieh: "You heard him because your window was open?"

Beverlee Sue: "Yes."

Ron Bamieh: "As you're looking at him, all you see is the back of his head."

Beverlee Sue: "Yes."

Ron Bamieh: "You could not see his face?"

Beverlee Sue: "That's correct."

Bamieh had her look at a diagram of the house and footbridge and describe what she saw.

Beverlee Sue: "He was urinating into the flower bed, which is like an L-shaped section against the front of the house."

Ron Bamieh: "When you talked to the grand jury in '97 you never mentioned the flower bed or the boy urinating, did you?"

Beverlee Sue: "No, but I didn't remember any of that at the time."

Ron Bamieh: "When you talked to Investigator Fitzgerald you didn't remember the boy urinating?"

Beverlee Sue: "No, I can't say he asked me any questions about that. Why don't you ask me what triggered it off so I can tell you and get this over with?"

Ron Bamieh: "So now you remember vividly, is that true?"

Beverlee Sue: "There was a chain of events that happened just recently that made me remember these things."

Ron Bamieh:[Pointing at the diagram] "How did you see him, ma'am?"

By this point Bamieh's voice had risen so high that he was shouting, and everyone chimed in at once, Wiksell, Beverlee Sue, and Judge O'Neill. Beverlee Sue yelled, "I didn't see his face, his back was to me!" Wiksell shouted, "Your Honor!" And Judge O'Neill joined the chorus, "Mr. Bamieh, your voice is getting too high at this time."

But Ron Bamieh ignored everyone and pressed on with Beverlee Sue, "Look at that diagram, ma'am. Where is your window?"

Beverlee Sue started to answer, "My window's right—" And then she noticed that it would be impossible for her to see a boy on the bridge from where her window was located. She said, "Oh, I did it backwards."

Now Bamieh was really shouting. "You didn't see anybody there!"

Beverlee Sue shouted back, "No, you're wrong!"

Wiksell said, "Your Honor!"

Judge O'Neill had enough. He proclaimed, "We're taking a break for fifteen minutes. Ladies and gentlemen of the jury, please keep in mind your admonitions and we'll see you in fifteen minutes."

When the jury was gone, Judge O'Neill turned to Bamieh and said, "Mr. Bamieh, I would just ask that you take control of your tone of voice, please. I know this is a very emotional situation, and that's understandable, but there have been two recent incidents so I'd like to keep things under control."

Bamieh answered, "I apologize."

After the break, Willard Wiksell tried to institute some damage control with Beverlee Sue Merriman on redirect. He showed Beverlee Sue the diagram again and she said, "I got the whole house turned around." She placed a large red *X* on the diagram where she said she had seen the bald-headed boy urinating off the footbridge.

Wiksell asked her, "What made you remember this individual on the bridge?"

Beverlee Sue answered, "Art Hernandez came to talk to me. I believe it was on the seventh of December and he asked me questions about [any of the boys on November 28, 1992] using the bathroom in the hallway. And I told him I would have heard them use the bathroom because of the water rush. But that clicked in the picture of why would [the boy] need to use the bathroom because he had already urinated off the bridge. And I saw the picture in my mind at that point."

Wiksell asked, "Are you making this up? Is this a last-minute lie to somehow help your son?"

Beverlee Sue answered, "No."

After this exchange, Bamieh took one more stab at her story about the boy on the bridge. He wanted to know why she went to such efforts to clean up blood and coffee stains in her house, but she never once mentioned about cleaning up urine from the patio area.

* * *

Finally it was time for closing arguments. While he summed up the case for the jury, Deputy DA Bamieh projected a sinister photo of Justin Merriman on a wall screen. The theme of his argument was of Justin Merriman as a man who committed a murder and had been on the run ever since. "The minute Justin Merriman raped Katrina Montgomery on November 28, 1992, he began running. He ran when he killed Montgomery because he thought she would rat on him. Ran from police, barricaded himself inside a house, and swung a knife at an officer before he was arrested. Ran when he tried to quiet and intimidate witnesses. Ran when he had his mother lie for him at his trial. Every step of the way, his behavior is consistent. And he's running and running and running and running."

In response Willard Wiksell tried to poke holes in Bamieh's case. And he did it by some unexpected means. In a complete reversal of his previous tactics, he conceded, to the surprise of almost everyone, that Justin Merriman had indeed murdered Katrina Montgomery, but it wasn't premeditated. Then he conceded that Merriman had tried to intimidate witnesses. But Wiksell vehemently denied that Merriman had raped anyone, including the other women who had come forward at trial.

Wiksell said, "Mr. Merriman probably never met a drug he didn't like. But he's not evil. Prosecutors proved the defendant ran from police and barricaded himself in a house on January 30, 1998, after officers tried to stop him from riding a bicycle without a rear reflector in west Ventura. And they proved Mr. Merriman wrote fellow gang members in early 1999 as part of a campaign to silence witnesses who testified during grand jury hearings that led to an indictment. Have the People proved a conspiracy beyond a reasonable doubt? Yeah. It's there. The prosecution proved its witness intimidation case. But when it comes to the rape allegations, Mr. Merriman is clearly not guilty. Two women who testified against him never reported the alleged assaults and both continued to hang out with Mr. Merriman. One of those women is a Skin Head Dogs girl. A party girl. Let's tell it like it is."

As for Ryan Bush and Larry Nicassio, Wiksell said they were both liars who sought a deal from the prosecution to save their own skins. "Both of them cried on cue, while on the stand, but both still have white supremacist and gang tattoos. Why would they bury the body if they weren't involved? They concealed evidence, stole money from her purse, and lied to the police. The prosecution's motive for murder is pure fiction. It's a case of second-degree murder and Bush and Nicassio are up to their ears in it."

Surprisingly, Wiksell saved some of his most scathing comments for his own witness, Beverlee Sue Merriman. He said, "She's a moron. She can't even recognize what antisocial idiots her son and friends are."

This garnered him a very dark look from Justin Merriman.

Wiksell went on to say, "Mr. Merriman had been drinking and using drugs during the party. He could not have formed the intent to kill. There is no evidence whatsoever that this was anything but an unconsidered, rash impulse, and if it is a rash impulse, it is not premeditated murder. He's guilty of second-degree murder and that's the way the case shakes out."

Before the jury went in for deliberation, Ron Bamieh had one more crack at them in rebuttal. He said, "Mr. Wiksell wants you to believe Mr. Bush and Mr. Nicassio about the murder, but not the rape. That's illogical. The case is a classic premeditated murder because Justin Merriman thought about what he would do before he did it. Even if you don't believe that, you should convict Mr. Merriman of first-degree murder because the killing occurred during a rape."

As for Wiksell's comments about this being second-degree murder, Bamieh said, "It's the last path they can take to run away from this. Don't let them take it."

It was now up to a jury of nine men and three women to decide whether Justin Merriman was guilty of first-degree murder, as well as an array of lesser charges. They'd been sitting through all of the testimony for over a month now, and it was with almost a sense of relief that they headed for the deliberation room. They deliberated for nearly ten hours before they gave the judge a message that they had reached a decision. On Tuesday, February 13, 2001, the jurors filed back into a packed courtroom. Almost every seat was taken. In fact, some of Katrina Montgomery's relatives and friends had to sit in each other's laps. In the front row, just behind Justin Merriman, his sister, Ember, and her husband waited in anticipation. One person glaringly absent from the courtroom was Beverlee Sue Merriman. She had been barred from attending by the judge.

When Judge Vincent O'Neill asked the jury foreperson how they found on the charge of murder, the spokesperson answered, "Guilty." The word "guilty" was pronounced eighteen more times on various lesser charges that dealt with rape and conspiracy. Justin Merriman was acquitted on only one charge of rape.

Merriman showed almost no reaction to the verdict. He leaned forward in his chair and then folded his arms. There was no lack of emotion in the Montgomery camp, however. Katy Montgomery cried out loud as soon as she heard the word "guilty" announced on the charge of first-degree murder. She dabbed her eyes with a Kleenex and later told a friend, "I told you. You remember, I told you? You have to trust God."

Ember Wyman gasped when she heard her brother's fate. After that, she and her husband left the courtroom without saying anything to reporters.

Outside the courtroom, Deputy DA Ron Bamieh was ecstatic. It had been a long hard road with many bumps along the way since he took on the case nearly four years before. He told reporters, "I'm proud of the way this office handled the case. A lot of people worked very hard for a long time with a lot of obstacles."

He especially dealt out praise to his investigators, Mark Volpei and Dennis Fitzgerald.

Defense attorney Willard Wiksell was naturally less enthused about the outcome, and he told reporters, "I'm disappointed but I respect the jury's decision. We saw the case as one where Nicassio and Bush were not believable, and the jury saw it otherwise."

As for changing tactics near the end of the trial and admitting that Merriman was guilty of second-degree murder and intimidation, but not rape and premeditated murder, Wiksell said that he wouldn't have changed a thing. "As the trial progressed, I think it became apparent that Mr. Merriman played a role in the death and disappearance of Ms. Montgomery. The only issue now is when does he die in jail? He cannot walk free again."

Indeed, that was the crux of the matter now. It would be up to the same jurors in the penalty phase as to whether Justin Merriman would die by lethal injection or spend the rest of his life in prison.

NINETEEN

THE WILD CARD

Before the jurors got a chance to decide whether Justin Merriman would die by lethal injection, there was an incident that threatened to derail everything and create a mistrial. Deputy David Kadosono, who had provided security throughout Justin Merriman's trial, bumped into Deputy Katie Baker at a local bookstore. In passing, she mentioned to him that she knew a juror and that juror had told her that [the jurors] were going "to fry Merriman." Deputy Baker had a brother who just happened to be married to the daughter of the juror in question.

Deputy Kadosono knew he was on very shaky ground. If he reported the incident, it could go badly for Baker. If he didn't report it, and it came out later, he might be in hot water himself. Finally Kadosono decided to tell Judge O'Neill and everything hit the fan.

It was discovered that Deputy Baker had also told her superiors in the sheriff's department, Captain Bruce Hansen and Sergeant Rick Barber, about the incident, and they never reported it to the court. This new threat to the validity of the trial pushed Ron Bamieh to the point of exasperation, and he told the press, "They jeopardized a case that took years to prepare. We're in the truth business. That is what we want from law enforcement."

The sheriff's department started an internal investigation and Chief Deputy Dante Honorico told a *Los Angles Times* reporter that the failure to report a conversation with a juror was against department policy. "It strikes at the heart of our integrity," he said, and he promised a full investigation that could lead to anything from a verbal reprimand to termination for Deputy Baker.

It was more than just a tempest in a teapot. Willard Wiksell and Phillip Capritto filed a motion for a mistrial. " 'We are going to fry him' means only one thing," Wiksell told reporters. "This jury should be thanked and excused. This whole penalty phase has been compromised. Mr. Merriman should be given a new trial [because] of the issue as to jury misconduct. It was apparent that the juror, and we know which one that is, did state she had a discussion outside of jury deliberation and prior to the verdict on the homicide being reached, in which she said that the jury was going to fry Mr. Merriman . . . It is clear that that is exactly what happened in this case. She made up her mind before. She made up her mind improperly and Mr. Merriman was not given the benefit of an impartial jury, which the Constitution guarantees."

Ron Bamieh argued just as vehemently that the jury had not been tainted, and in one regard, he was in luck. The juror in question had recently been excused because of an unrelated illness in her family. And apparently none of the other jurors knew about her conversation with Deputy Baker.

After taking the matter under advisement, Judge O'Neill said the defense's motion was denied. He pointed out that the remark "have him fry" was actually initiated by Deputy Baker, in her hopes that the jury would find Merriman guilty. And the juror had responded that she thought the death penalty would be imposed. But those remarks did not prejudice other jurors.

Trying another area, Merriman's defense lawyers hit the issue of fairness that Justin should be facing the death penalty while Larry Nicassio got just three years and Ryan Bush no time at all. They brought a motion to reduce the penalty to life without the possibility of parole.

Willard Wiksell said, "Your Honor, I would like to point out that under the People's theory, there were three people supposedly, and I say supposedly, in the Merriman room that night. Two people, Mr. Nicassio and Mr. Bush, have walked away absolutely free. Both of those people received deals from the prosecution. They're walking around now. They're free. They're free to live their lives. I sense an imbalance here, a fundamental unfairness, that the only one left holding the bag is Mr. Merriman.

"I am not going to go over all the evidence, this is not what we do here, but I think it's important to remind the court that the testimony is that Mr. Nicassio came up behind Miss Montgomery with a knife, the evidence was that he put a knife at her throat. Mr. Bush had a knife. Mr. Bush and Nicassio buried this body without Mr. Merriman being present. They moved the body, hid it in a place only they knew.

"They were involved in her disappearance. They stole her money. They bought clothes with her money. Nicassio and Bush are cousins. They were up to their ears . . . they were well over their ears in the homicide of Miss Montgomery.

"Now, what I'm suggesting by my statements here is that it is fundamentally unfair that Mr. Merriman receive the death penalty, and the imbalance is that these two people walk away totally free.

"In my view, if Mr. Bamieh and the district attorney's office of this county would have decided that Mr. Nicassio was responsible, without question he would be convicted of murder.

"The fact they can sit here and say that they just don't believe that he was responsible . . . I certainly think if they decided to prosecute him, he would have been convicted. The same with Mr. Bush. People every day are convicted on these facts in this county as well as every county, throughout the United States.

"Just to sum it up, the reason I am asking the court to reduce the penalty is that there's two people walking around free who could easily have been convicted and served a life term in the Department of Corrections."

Ron Bamieh was right back at him with, "What's fundamentally unfair is that the defendant raped Miss Montgomery repeatedly that evening. What's fundamentally unfair is that she was slaughtered by the defendant. What's fundamentally unfair is that the defendant raped five other women. He's a serial rapist. What's fundamentally unfair is that the aggravating factors on this defendant are probably more severe than most defendants who face this penalty. Mr. Wiksell's view of the evidence is completely skewed and was rejected, and the theories he presented at trial were also rejected. It wasn't the People who said Mr. Nicassio was not liable for the murder, it was the evidence. And part of that evidence was the defendant's own statement to Mr. Nicassio telling him that [Nicassio] was not liable for the murder. So the reality is we are sitting here with a rapist, a serial rapist and a cold-blooded murderer. In this state we do have the death penalty. It is reserved for the most heinous crimes and the most heinous defendants. And the person over there in blue sitting to my right fits that description and this court should impose that penalty."

* * *

The penalty phase of the trial began near the end of February 2001. It started with the emotional outpouring of grief from various members of the Montgomery family about their pain and loss.

Katrina's grandmother Jean Montgomery said, "This was my granddaughter's first prayer:

> Now I lay me down to sleep,
> I pray the Lord my soul to keep.
> If I die before I wake,
> I pray the Lord my soul to take.

"Justin Merriman did not allow Katrina to utter her last prayer. I cannot forgive Justin Merriman. We waited for Katrina to show up in Santa Barbara. But she never arrived."

Katrina's father, Michael, said, "We remember Trina with the aid of videos, home movies, photographs, and hundreds of loving cousins, second cousins, and friends. The most difficult times have been holidays. There is a giant void in my life and in the life of my family, and as a result you tend to want the holidays to go by quickly because it's a constant reminder of our loss.

"People talked about time healing, and I do acknowledge that there is a truth in that, in that I have lost my father and my wife's parents, who I was very close with, and time has healed that loss. Unfortunately, I fear that under the circumstances in which we lost Trina, knowing the terror and agony she suffered in her last minutes on this earth, I fear there will never ever be any healing.

"There are so many days that I would come home from my distraction of work and could see the expression on my wife's face and realize she had never gotten out of bed that day. Literally, she had to pick herself up day in and day out to deal with the loss of our daughter.

"Because of my career, I was less close with my daughter than my wife was. My wife and my daughter were best of friends, and this loss shattered my wife. She always had a sparkle in her eyes, and that I haven't seen in eight years.

"I wanted to tell you today that what you have seen of my daughter in this trial is such a small, small piece of her life. She was bright, witty, she inherited my father-in-law's cutting-edge dry sense of humor, and she was always, always energetic, friendly, and courteous.

"I don't know of an incident in her life where I was present where she was ever unkind or rude to anyone. That doesn't mean she didn't tear people apart with her cutting-edge humor. And she thought she was smarter than everyone, and in the end, I believe that may have been her undoing. It fostered a sense of invincibility on her part, which, in my mind, is the only explanation for why she made the poor choices she made on that fateful evening of November of 1992."

Katy Montgomery cried through much of her testimony. "Trina kind of acted out when she was around fifteen or sixteen. But she had so much respect for family and what family meant, that she never really showed that side to her aunts and uncles. Especially her grandparents. She was always the perfect sweet loving Trina. They knew we were going through such a hard time and they didn't understand why. Trina? She'd never be like that."

Ron Bamieh projected home videos of Katrina and her family and extended family on a screen. It contained videos of Christmas 1990, a wedding, and her grandparents' anniversary.

Bamieh asked Katy Montgomery, "The first one, Christmas of '90, and people were singing 'Happy Birthday.' Do you remember that day?"

Katy replied, "Yeah. My sister Tina was born on Christmas Day so we always sing happy birthday to her on Christmas."

Bamieh asked, "On that other one, where Trina was dancing out there, what was that?"

Katy answered, "That was my brother Tony's wedding that we were all at. It's her dancing with her cousin Tommy and the little cousins dancing with each other."

Bamieh said, "And the last video we saw, I saw her walking in a green dress there as you look at it on the right side of the screen. Do you remember that event?"

Montgomery answered, "That was my outfit. That was my parents' fiftieth wedding anniversary that we sang to them at. All my brothers and sisters and then all of our children joining us for the end of the song."

"I take it your family still has similar types of events where you all get together to celebrate things. At those times, do you feel Trina's absence?"

Katy replied, "Always. There's so many of us, but she's always missing. It's so hard sometimes because she's frozen right at twenty. And I see her best friend, Lee, and her cousins getting older and getting married and having children. It's so joyous and I'm so happy for them, but it's like she'll never have that, you know. She'll always be missing."

Bamieh asked, "Over the time she's been gone, have you had a funeral for her?"

Katy cried, "No. In the beginning we kept thinking that . . . even when we knew she wasn't alive anymore, we kept thinking they would find her body. Even if we didn't know what happened. But they never have.

"And then we just kept waiting and we hoped that even if she wasn't found that it would finally go to trial, and we would know the truth about what happened and the person responsible would be held accountable. And we just waited for so long, and at one point we started talking about doing a service, but people thought, who really didn't know, that we were giving up hope. Like she was magically out there or something. And it just seemed so wrong to think perhaps she was alive and we were gonna do this service or something.

"So we just waited all this time. But now we're gonna do one. Now we're really gonna do one.

"What you've seen in this courtroom is what happened to her, but it's not who she was at all. And it's been eight years, focusing on the ugly circumstances of what happened to her, with people that didn't love her and know her. It's been so difficult. So we're finally able to really have it be about Trina and who she was and all her wonderful qualities. And how much we loved her. We can finally say good-bye to her in the way that she's always deserved.

"We thank God that what was kept hidden for eight years has been exposed to the light of truth in this courtroom. What needed to be said has been said and what needed to be done has been done. We have endured all that we are able and we trust the court to bring this to a just end today."

If those who spoke for Justin Merriman's death by lethal injection were emotional in their delivery, those who spoke for him spending the rest of his life in prison were dispassionate and clinical. Dr. Leonard Diamond, who had seen Justin Merriman when he was seventeen years old, told how he had warned the authorities back then what would happen if Justin did not receive treatment. "I indicated that he was headed for some serious trouble. I recommended that he be confined to the California Youth Authority and receive treatment for a personality disorder. I felt he was a significant danger to the people of the state of California. But he never got the treatment he needed. In less than a year he was moved to state prison after attacking a CYA guard."

Then Dr. Diamond spoke of another meeting with Justin Merriman he had attended at Willard Wiksell's request. This had happened only two months before. Diamond said, "[Merriman] has changed very little. He was hostile, suspicious, and exhibiting blatant stupidity. He is deficient in all ways. He says and does the wrong things consistently. During the exam I asked him to draw a house, a tree, and a person. For the person he drew a forty-four-year-old cartoon character named Fred who screams when he gets upset."

Dr. Diamond tried to show that Merriman had, in effect, not grown up into anything resembling a normal adult. He still remained a rebellious adolescent with a low IQ, incapable of making rational decisions.

Even more graphic than Diamond's testimony was that of UC Irvine psychiatrist Dr. Joseph Wu. Dr. Wu had performed a brain scan recently on Justin Merriman and found an abnormal pattern consistent with a possible brain injury. Dr. Wu thought Merriman might have suffered this at birth. In his estimation, Merriman had a very low IQ. Dr. Wu showed jurors photographs from a videotape of Justin Merriman's brain. Instead of a peach-colored normal brain, Merriman's brain had bright red and green areas consistent with abnormality. Particularly disturbing to Dr. Wu was the scan of Merriman's brain that showed his frontal lobe. According to Dr. Wu, there was much lower activity there than in a normal brain. The frontal lobe is an area that controls aggression, judgment, and impulse controls.

During rebuttal, Ron Bamieh hammered back at Dr. Wu's findings, accusing him of selling himself to defense attorneys to bring money into the coffers of UC Irvine. He noted that Dr. Wu received $490 an hour for his work.

* * *

At this point, it should have been a contest between the emotionalism of the Montgomery family and the clinical statements of the doctors. But there was a wild card in the mix, and the wild card was Justin Merriman. Against the strong advice of his defense attorney, Willard Wiksell, Justin Merriman demanded to take the stand to speak in his own penalty phase.

Wiksell told the judge, "If there was any way I could keep him off the stand, I would, Your Honor."

Judge O'Neill asked Merriman if he was sure he wanted to do this.

Merriman said, "I already talked to [Wiksell]. I'm ready to go."

With Beverlee Sue Merriman now in attendance, along with Ember and Justin's grandmother, Justin Merriman took the stand to address the jurors. But what happened next took everyone by surprise. As Merriman was sworn in he kept raising his arm higher and higher until he was giving a full-fledged Nazi salute.

Reporter Aron Miller, who had sat through the entire trial, said, "I couldn't believe it. The whole courtroom was absolutely stunned."

With his arm extended, Merriman finished the oath and said, "So help me God."

When he began to speak, it became apparent right away why one of his gang nicknames was Mumbles. He indeed mumbled into the microphone and tapped it, saying, "Check, check."

Then he said, "There's a few things I want to bring up, Your Honor. I thought last time we were in court I gave a letter to him, to my brother [another gang member] right there in the audience, and I never heard back from him. I wrote a ten-page letter to my sister. I'm just wondering if I could ask them about my mail 'cause I haven't heard back from either one of them. I don't know if Mr. Bamieh is playing his game still with my mail, or you know . . . I just wanted to bring that up or you could ask him."

Judge O'Neill said to Ron Bamieh, "Refresh my memory."

Bamieh said, "The People provided the court with letters that Mr. Merriman was piggybacking . . . to other people. He took those letters out and mailed them through his sister. But this issue . . . it's kind of like Mrs. Lincoln talking about the play [after President Lincoln had just been shot]. I'm not really in the mood to have a hearing on that at this time. It's kind of ridiculous when what is going on is going on."

Merriman shot back, "What's ridiculous is him playing little games with my mail and coming before you and everybody in this courtroom and lying. That's ridiculous. It might be ridiculous to him, but not to me. This is my only form of communication for the last three years I've been in the hole."

Judge O'Neill refused to have a hearing on the letter issue, so Justin Merriman continued.

"Ladies and gentlemen, I would like to take a few moments of your time to address a few issues briefly before I get sentenced. I would first like to thank my family for their ongoing love and support through all that has transpired here at this courthouse. I know this is the hardest thing you have ever had to do or ever will have to go through in your life. I want to tell you that I love you with all my heart and I always have and most definitely will. Due to your strong love and dedication, I am able to deal with this great unjustice life has handed down upon me.

"As I sit and ponder all that has taken place, I can't believe the outcome that has ultimately become my fate in life. Yes, I'm the first to acknowledge the fact that I have not been no angel in my youthful days. But those things were paid for and does this justify taking my life away? For that is exactly what you are doing.

"Whether it be life in prison or death, this sentence is death and it's being justified by a whole lot of lies the prosecution side, in its effort to win their case by means of making plenty of deals with known felons that would do almost anything or say anything to protect their safety as well as their freedom.

"Practically every person testifying on behalf of the prosecution either willfully came to or was approached with propositions of favors in return for favors.

"Last week I worked on three pages I was going to add to what I said. It was completely smashing my attorney Bill Wiksell. Things I felt should have been done in my defense. But after reading it again . . . I was frustrated with the way things transpired during the proceedings and my trial and not being able to do anything about it.

"Still, to this minute on this day, I feel there should have been more done on my case. Like people to be called for my defense. Which means Mr. Wiksell would have had to send out some investigators. And that did not happen in my case.

"But you know, I'm still grateful for the things he has done for me before and during my trial.

"I thank Mr. Wiksell, along with cocounsel Phillip Capritto and both investigators, Fred De Fazio and Art Hernandez, for what they've done.

"Now I would like to address some issues on behalf of the lead prosecutor Ronald Bamieh, who throughout the trial I feel acted very unprofessional with his blatant, immature, and derogatory remarks such as disrepectful name-calling in the courtroom.

"Another thing was a statement in court as well as in the

L.A. *Times* article being as, 'We're in the truth business. That is what we want from law enforcement.'

"He has made these statements and yet has continued to lie constantly during motions before my trial, also during statements throughout my trial and even went as far as putting words in his own witnesses' testimony.

"I mean, I would love to sit up here and have a bagging contest between me and him. We'd have fun. I could think of some good ones for you all day long. He said that the jury misconduct was solved because the juror was taken off the case and there was no evidence as to whether the other jurors have made up their minds. If that was the case, then the juror would have been quoted as saying, 'I am going to fry him.' But she was quoted as saying, 'We are going to fry him.' The word 'we' is meaning more than one. As in, 'we the jury.'

"Therefore, the statement by Mr. Bamieh as to this issue being resolved is wrong. It is not only obvious this juror had her mind made up prior to deliberations, but by the wording of her statement she has obviously had discussions with one or more of the other jurors. Therefore, yes, the jury is and was prejudicial and therefore holds grounds for a mistrial.

"There are too many things I've wanted to comment on during court but I kept quiet. But this is something I have said before and I will continue saying it, for it is the truth. I stand before you in complete innocence. I have a lot of people who know for a fact I am innocent of these crimes. My life has been taken away unjustly. I want the Montgomery family and friends to know I did not do these crimes. I did not take your beloved from you. I am not the person I've been made out to be. I am truly sorry for your loss. I can see your pain and the thoughts and your feelings for me, as well. Like I said before, Trina was a very bright young lady with a wonderful heart and will be missed by many, and by me, as well.

"That's all. Thank you."

* * *

After Merriman's soliloquy on the stand, Ron Bamieh attempted to ask Merriman some questions. But Merriman just glowered at him and said, "I'm not answering any questions from nobody, especially not someone working for the district attorney's office or anyone in law enforcement."

"I just want to ask you about how you killed Katrina Montgomery," Bamieh said.

"I'm sorry about what happened, but I did not kill her."

Bamieh shot back, "So you get up here and say your piece and now you're going to be a coward and refuse to answer my questions?"

Merriman just glared back at him and folded his arms.

Bamieh went on to portray Merriman to the jurors as "bad rather than just brain-damaged. Why don't we just accept the fact there are some people who consistently commit evil acts? The explanation is not that he has brain injury or ADHD [Attention Deficit Hyperactivity Disorder]. The explanation is that his is e-v-i-l."

Willard Wiksell followed Bamieh with a plea for mercy, noting that Justin Merriman would spend the rest of his life in prison. "He won't be able to pick up a kitten or touch a Christmas ornament. On February thirteenth [the date of his conviction], he died. It's over."

Then, as Willard Wiksell spoke of Merriman's consensual sex that had turned unconsensual, Justin Merriman suddenly interrupted him and said, "I object!"

"You do?" Wiksell asked in stunned amazement.

"You cannot object," Judge O'Neill told Merriman.

A few minutes later, when Wiksell mentioned rape again, Merriman objected for a second time. Merriman said, "Your Honor, I don't want to listen to this anymore. There was nothing unconsensual about those encounters."

Ron Bamieh was incensed by Merriman's latest antics and he asked Judge O'Neill to toss Merriman out of the courtroom. Judge O'Neill didn't go that far, but he admonished Merriman not to speak up again.

Reporter Aron Miller, who had sat through almost all of the jury trial, noted that Justin Merriman often seemed more upset by the rape charges than he did about the murder charge. "He didn't seem to get it," Miller said, " that the charge of murder in the first degree was more serious than the rape charge. He had a fixation about not being called a rapist. In some regards, he had murdered Katrina Montgomery just so she wouldn't tell that he had raped her. He was absolutely obsessed with not having the label 'rapist' placed on him."

Justin Merriman certainly hadn't helped his cause by exhibiting the Nazi salute or disrupting the court with objections. When the jury returned with a verdict on sentencing, the courtroom was absolutely packed. Beverlee Sue Merriman and Ember Wyman sat in the front row right behind Justin's chair. He sat stone-faced as the jurors slowly filed in.

Judge O'Neill was passed the verdict and he gazed at Merriman twice, once when he said his name, and the other when he uttered the words, "Justin Merriman, for the offense of murder of Katrina Montgomery as charged in Count One of the indictment of which you were previously found guilty, the jury having found the offense of murder to be of the first degree and the jury having found special circumstances of forcible rape and forcible oral copulation were true . . . it is the judgment of this court that you shall suffer the death penalty. Said penalty is to be inflicted within the walls of the state prison at San Quentin, California, in the manner prescribed by law and at a time to be fixed by this court in a warrant of execution."

Justin Merriman leaned forward in his chair and then began slowly rocking back and forth, not saying a word.

Katrina Montgomery's parents hugged each other as Beverlee Sue Merriman glared at the judge and stalked out of the courtroom, just as silent as her son. Only Ember, his sister, agreed to talk with reporters. She said, "This is very difficult. But I love him. I love my brother."

Willard Wiksell was upset, as well. "It was very difficult to sit through these proceedings," he said. "It's disappointing."

Disappointment was not the order of the day on the other side. Outside the courtroom, Michael Montgomery thanked Deputy DA Kevin Drescher, Investigator Mark Volpei, Investigator Dennis Fitzgerald, and especially Deputy DA Ron Bamieh. He told reporters, "It's a fair and appropriate sentence. Our family takes no joy in the fact this jury has sentenced Justin Merriman to death. It will not bring our daughter back."

District Attorney Bradley commented, "This is one case where justice delayed was not justice denied. If this doesn't warrant the death penalty, no case does."

Perhaps the person most satisfied with the sentence was Deputy DA Ron Bamieh. The entire ordeal for him had lasted four years and had gone down unexpected and uncharted roads. He'd been forced to look at a dark side of Ventura County he barely knew existed when he began the process. But in the end, he and his investigators broke the back of the Skin Head Dogs street gang. By March 2001, many of its members were in prison and there was almost no vitality left among those still on the streets. In essence, they had torn themselves apart by informing and wearing wires. Justin Merriman had been a big reason for their downfall.

Ron Bamieh said, "Justin Merriman is disgusting and pathetic. Frankly, he scares me. Ventura County is now safer."

MORE MUST-READ TRUE CRIME
FROM PINNACLE